In Our Hands

A Peace and Social Justice Program
Senior High

Eleanor Hunting

Virginia Lane

Harold Rosen

with

Barry Andrews, Robert C. Branch, Samuel Goldenberg,

Pat Hoertdoerfer, Mary Thomson

David Marshak, Developmental Editor

Judith Frediani, Project Editor

A Project of the Peace and Social Justice Curriculum Team

Unitarian Universalist Association

Permission is granted to photocopy all the Handouts, the session posters in Session 3, and the "Profiles" and "Panel Questions" in Session 8.

Production Editor: Kathy Wolff
Text Designer: Suzanne Morgan
Cover Designer: Lisa Clark
Editorial Assistant: Timothy Reynolds
Cover Art: Dr. Charlie Clements Peace Quilt © Boise
     Peace Quilt Project. Used by permission.

Acknowledgments

We want to thank Mary Madison for her contribution to the work of the Peace and Social Justice Curriculum Team during her tenure on the team in 1984-85.

We wish to acknowledge the significant contribution made to the development of this program by the youth and leaders who took part in the curriculum's field test. These field testers were members of the following congregations: the Northwest Unitarian Congregation of Atlanta, GA; the Unitarian Universalist Church of Muncie, IN; the First Unitarian Church of Toledo, OH; and the Michael Servetus Unitarian Universalist Fellowship of Vancouver, WA.

We are grateful for the contribution made to the development of this program by Pamela Vinicombe, executive director of the Murray Grove Center, through her helpful critique of the curriculum.

"My World," the poem by Josephine Panayiota, is printed here with permission from Exley Publications. Use of "And Then...," by Judy Chicago, and "What Will Be the Shape of My Future?" by R. Carroll Cannon, is gratefully acknowledged.

Finally, we want to thank members of the UUA's Religious Education Department and members of the UUA Religious Education Advisory Committee for their important contributions to this program.

Contents

Introduction to *In Our Hands*

"We, the member congregations of the Unitarian Universalist Association, covenant to affirm and promote: the inherent worth and dignity of every person; justice, equity, and compassion in human relations...."

So begins the Principles and Purposes covenant adopted by the Unitarian Universalist Association in 1985. The statement underscores the denomination's deep commitment to justice, a commitment that marks the history of the two liberal religious traditions, Unitarianism and Universalism.

Unitarian Universalists celebrate and remember a worthy collection of forebears who struggled for peace and justice. We remember Benjamin Rush and his timely defense of social equality in the late eighteenth century. We remember Theodore Parker's passion for abolition a generation later. We celebrate Adin Ballou's powerful critique of industrial society, Clara Barton, founder of the American Red Cross, and William Ellery Channing's abhorrence of poverty. We remember Dorothea Dix, reformer of prisons and psychiatric hospitals, and Susan B. Anthony, eminently successful suffragist. We honor Olympia Brown, Jane Addams, Elizabeth Blackwell, and Albert Schweitzer.

In more recent history, we celebrate the contributions of John Haynes Holmes, pacifist, human rights advocate, and co-founder of the War Resisters' League and the American Civil Liberties Union. And Donald Thompson, shot as he stood up for civil rights in Jackson, Mississippi, in the early 1960s. We remember James Reeb, beaten to death for the same cause on the streets of Selma, Alabama in 1965 and Whitney Young, Jr., head of the National Urban League. We celebrate, too, the Unitarian Universalist Association's decision to publish the controversial Pentagon Papers despite government harassment, and the Association's long-standing commitment to gay and lesbian civil rights.

We celebrated the Unitarian Universalist Service Committee's fiftieth anniversary in 1989. The UUSC has worked at home to fund minority-directed community projects, and abroad to enable people to gain control over their political, economic, and social institutions. The UUSC has sponsored many fact-finding missions to Central America to publicize human rights violations. The UUSC has its roots in Unitarian and Universalist service committees that aided World War II refugees and led humanitarian efforts throughout the world.

Grounded in this rich history, present-day Unitarian Universalists have a commitment to peace and justice that must look forward, not back. With the inspiration of such activists, we must live our lives as peacemakers and champions of fair play.

In Our Hands is a manifestation of our belief in ourselves, our children, and our future. The Peace and Social Justice Curriculum Team began its work in November, 1983 and finished in November, 1988. The team consisted primarily of Unitarian Universalists from the Pacific Northwest of the United States and British Columbia, Canada. The team developed five religious education curricula: programs for children from five to nine years old, from nine to twelve years, for junior-high age, for senior-high age, and for adults.

The team articulated the following statement, which has served as the philosophical center in the development of its curricula.

Peace and Social Justice Education for Unitarian Universalists: A Rationale

The Present Crisis

The most serious issues facing the world today are issues of peace and justice. The nuclear arms race, tyranny, hunger, poverty, torture, terrorism, even pollution and depletion of the world's resources are all problems of peace and justice. At the same time, although the magnitude and urgency of these problems is unprecedented in human history, issues of peace and justice have always been central concerns of human beings.

Linking Peace and Justice

Peace and justice are necessarily interdependent. Each requires the other. Real peace is not possible without justice. Injustice is the result of violence, which is often institutionalized as exploitation and oppression. Injustice is also a cause of violence in the form of criminal behavior, rebellion, and in reprisal, repression. In addition, true justice is not possible without peace. As long as individuals or groups are engaged in threats or acts of aggression, others are deprived of basic human rights, including freedom, equality, and life itself. Thus, peace and justice are both integral to the definition of the other. Peace is the achieving of justice, cooperation, and nonviolence. Justice is the realization of peace, freedom, and equality. Both peace and justice are necessary conditions for human fulfillment.

Ends and Means, Ideals and Realities

Peace and justice are at once ideal goals and actual processes. The vision of a just and peaceful world offers a stimulus for action and a standard by which to judge our efforts. As an actual process, however, peace and justice are always partial and never complete realizations of the ideal goal. Peace and justice are integral parts of the process by which the goals are sought. The means for achieving peace and justice must be congruent with the ends of peace and justice.

Moreover, even as ideal goals, peace and justice must not be viewed as states of perfect accord. A just and peaceful world will not be without disagreement and conflict or the exercise of power. The realization of peace and justice thus requires the nonviolent resolution of disagreement and conflict. It also requires an exercise of power by individuals and institutions that is characterized by and in the service of the ideals of peace and justice.

Cherishing the Earth

Peace and justice include an ecological dimension. The earth is our only source of material sustenance, as well as a major source of our spiritual nurturance. Degradation and destruction of the earth are inherently violent and lead to increasing conflict and injustice. Peace and justice require a reverence for the earth and an understanding of human interdependence, both material and spiritual, with the rest of nature.

Defining Peace and Justice

As an ideal goal, peace and justice are characterized by a set of relationships that describe both absence and presence:

- The *absence* of uncontrolled violence within the individual's psyche; and the *presence* of a sense of wholeness, self-worth, and empowerment within the individual's psyche; the acceptance of inner conflict and the ability to work with such conflict toward growth and integration.
- The *absence* of interpersonal violence; and the *presence* of interpersonal justice, in which justice is defined as fairness and respect due to each person by right and is based upon nonviolence, effective communication, conflict resolution, and cooperation; and the presence of basic political rights, such as freedom and equality, and basic social and economic rights, such as food, health care, employment, and education.
- The *absence* of violence among people of different nations, religions, and cultures; and the *presence* of justice among people of different nations, religions, and cultures, based upon nonviolence, effective communication, conflict resolution, and cooperation.
- The *absence* of destruction of the natural environment; and the *presence* of reverence for nature, and human behavior guided both by this reverence and by an understanding of our status as a part of nature and our interdependence with the rest of the natural world.

The ideal of peace and justice is dependent on four kinds of interrelated relationships:

- among the various parts of the individual's psyche (intrapersonal);
- between and among people (interpersonal);
- between and among institutions of governance and religious faith (inter-institutional); and
- between each individual and nature (global).

As we consider peace and justice as a process, not an ideal goal, we must see these characteristics not in terms of absolutes but in terms of their relative absence or presence.

Peace and Justice Education

The objective of peace and justice education is peace-and-justice making (or peacemaking and justice-building). It engages people to stimulate and encourage their development as makers of peace and justice: within their own psyches, in their relationships with others, in their roles as citizens of a nation and members of a religious group, and in their identification as humans living on the earth.

Sources of Authority

Unitarian Universalists derive their authority for peace–and–justice making from several sources:

- their individual commitments to helping create peace and justice on this planet;
- their reverence for life;
- the Principles and Purposes of the Unitarian Universalist Association, adopted in 1985:

    —The inherent worth and dignity of every person
    —Justice, equity, and compassion in human relations
    —The right of conscience and the use of the democratic process within our congregations and in society at large
    —The goal of world community with peace, liberty, and justice for all
    —Respect for the interdependent web of existence of which we are a part.

In Our Hands is a product of our history of commitment to peace and justice over the centuries, as exemplified by Unitarian Universalist heroines and heroes, including members of our own congregations and families; and our understanding and appreciation of the world's religions, all of which teach a version of "the golden rule."

Introduction to *Senior High*

In Our Hands: Senior High is a 12-session religious education program for people in grades 10 through 12, or approximately 15 to 18 years old. It is designed for a minimum group size of four or five. After the three introductory sessions, participants choose which of Sessions 4 through 11 they would like to experience. The program concludes with Session 12.

In Our Hands: Senior High involves high school youth in considering the nature and meaning of peace and social justice. They are invited to explore some or all of the following topics and issues: the nature of conflict, and conflict management and resolution; paths to peace and justice; common Unitarian Universalist faith-stances and their relationship to peace and justice; peace-makers and justice-builders; critical peace and justice issues; the ways in which people act for peace and justice; and Unitarian Universalist worship for peace and justice. Participants are also invited to plan and carry out both a social education, service, witness, or action project and a peace and justice worship service for their congregation. The program closes with an opportunity for participants to reflect on what they have experienced, make meaning of their activities in this group, and celebrate their accomplishments and learning.

Principles and Goals

In Our Hands: Senior High is centered on five of the Principles and Purposes adopted by the Unitarian Universalist Association in 1985, as follows:

We, the member congregations of the Unitarian Universalist Association, covenant to affirm and promote:

- The inherent worth and dignity of every person;
- Justice, equity, and compassion in human relations;
- The right of conscience and the use of the democratic process;
- The goal of world community with peace, liberty, and justice for all;
- Respect for the interdependent web of all existence of which we are a part.

Overall goals for participants are:

- to develop a greater understanding of and a deeper feeling for a variety of peace and justice issues
- to gain insight into and understanding of their own attitudes and beliefs about peace and justice
- to gain familiarity with the social responsibility programs and groups within their congregation, community, district, and throughout the denomination
- to increase their willingness to act in support of these ideals
- to deepen their commitment to peace and justice as religious and practical ideals.

Depending on their choice of sessions, participants can also fulfill some or all the following goals:

- to learn skills for conflict management and creative conflict resolution
- to understand four paths to peace and justice taken by individuals and societies: strength, diplomacy, law, and spiritual nonviolence
- to gain a greater understanding of four common Unitarian Universalist faith-stances and the relationships between these faith-stances and peace and justice issues
- to enrich their knowledge of the lives of several effective peace-makers and justice-builders
- to deepen their understanding of and feeling for several critical peace and justice issues that confront the lives of human beings on this planet
- to explore Unitarian Universalist worship and/or social education, service, witness, and action as ways to act for peace and justice
- to enact projects that provide experience in planning and carrying out these kinds of activities.

Program Structure

In Our Hands: Senior High begins with two introductory sessions that engage participants in exploring their beliefs, attitudes, understandings, and feelings about a variety of peace and justice issues. In Session 3, participants survey Sessions 4 through 11 and choose the sessions they wish to experience.

Once this selection has been made, the group continues with the chosen sessions as well as any additional projects and activities that participants wish to undertake.

The program concludes with a series of culminating activities in Session 12.

Session Structure

Each session is organized in the following sequence:

Gathering: Introducing the topic(s); stimulating thinking and feeling about the topic(s); engaging the participants.

Interacting: Engaging the participants in examining the topic(s); encouraging participants to articulate what they know and feel about the topic(s); evoking active participation from all.

Investigating: Exploring new ideas, information, concepts, understandings, and skills; considering the meanings, significance, implications of new ideas, information, and perspectives.

Integrating: Making sense of what has been explored; considering implications for action, future investigation.

Closing: Closing with a repeated ritual.

Session Length

Sessions are planned for 60 to 75 minutes, a length that is suitable for both a Sunday morning high school program and an evening or afternoon youth group program.

If possible, arrange to have 75-minute sessions. With an evening youth group program, you can devote 75 minutes to the activities of this curriculum and the remaining time to the group's other affairs. With a Sunday morning meeting time, you can add 15 minutes to the schedule either by starting 15 minutes prior to the congregation's worship service, or by ending 15 minutes later.

If you have only 60 minutes for each meeting, you can still complete the sessions as planned, but be aware of your time and keep the activities moving along briskly.

Leaders

We strongly recommend a pair of co-leaders for this program. Co-leadership provides a richer experience for the participants by giving them two or more adults with whom they can develop positive and trusting relationships.

Co-leadership also provides significant benefits for the adult leaders. Co-leaders don't feel isolated from the congregation, because they are working with another member of the congregation. Co-leaders can share experiences and give each other helpful feedback. Through these interactions, they can help each other gain increasing competence and skill. They might also develop a friendship! Co-leadership also lessens the pressure on any one leader to attend every session. With co-leaders, each leader can miss a session or two during the course of the program without feeling that this will cause a significant disruption for the participants.

The Nature of Your Group: New or Ongoing?

This program can be used with both newly formed and ongoing senior high groups. If your group has already been "built," you can begin with Session 1 as written. If your group is new, it is important to build the group to some extent before beginning this program.

Some suggestions for group-building:

- Use nametags for the first several sessions, so that participants learn each others' names.
- Devote part or all of the first sessions to activities designed to help participants get to know each other and begin to feel trust in you and in this group. For examples of these activities, see Unit I in *Life Issues for Teenagers* (*LIFT*, Boston: UUA, 1985).
- Early in the program, engage the group in a social activity and/or field trip to build good feeling and a sense of connection among the participants.

Environment

Senior high groups enjoy meeting in a space for which they feel a sense of ownership. Participants develop this sense by furnishing and decorating the space.

It is desirable to have a space that is comfortable, large enough for the activities of this program, clean and aesthetically pleasing, and free from distractions.

Leader Preparation

One way to prepare to lead sessions is:

1. Read over the session plan.
2. Read it again, jotting down brief notes about each activity on a notecard.
3. Do the preparation needed for the session.
4. Use the notecard you have prepared to guide you as you lead the session.

Approximate Times

Each activity is accompanied by an approximate time, usually expressed as a range. These approximate times give you information about how much time the various activities require for successful enactment. The actual time required can vary considerably depending on group size, the characteristics of the group, and leadership style.

Thus, the times are suggestions and approximations, not requirements or limitations of any kind. Be sensitive to the energies and interests of your participants as they engage in each activity. At the same time, lead your group through a session plan in such a way that each activity receives appropriate attention.

Setting Up Your Resource Table

In Our Hands: Senior High asks you to create a Resource Table that includes a wide variety of print material and visuals relating to peace and justice activities, issues, organizations, and projects. The Resource Table can be an effective way to make participants aware of what is taking place in relation to peace and justice issues in your congregation, community, region, and nation.

Invite participants to bring in materials for the Resource Table. Ask for resources from members of your congregation who are active in the Unitarian Universalist Service Committee, the Unitarian Universalist Peace Network, the Unitarian Universalist United Nations Organization, and other UU-related organizations active in peace and social justice efforts. Your congregational social responsibility committee and members of local and national peace and justice organizations may also have print materials to contribute.

Try to add new material to the table for each session.

Checking-In

After Session 1, each session begins with a brief checking-in activity. Checking-in is an opportunity for people to share a little about what is going on in their lives: experiences during the past week, high and low points, ideas and feelings relating to this program, and so on.

Create a checking-in process that is open and sharing, but also relatively brief.

Rules for Sharing

Establish a norm of respect for each other and each other's expression within the group. As much as possible, elicit the articulation and support of this norm from the participants.

If the group is ongoing, you probably have dealt with this issue already and need only review its importance.

If the group is new, explore the concept of respect with the participants during your first meeting. Engage people in discussing the value of respect in a group such as this and the destructive effects of sarcasm, "put-downs," and so on.

Closing

Each session concludes with a closing in which participants share a common ritual. The Closing gives participants an opportunity to reflect on their experience of that session and reinforce their feelings of connection and cohesion with each other.

Note that the first session plans provide detailed closing activities. Most of the subsequent plans suggest one or two activities and then ask you to design an appropriate closing for your group.

Create closings that fit the nature of your group. Use singing, holding hands in a circle, and other activities if your participants are comfortable with them.

Using the "Reflection and Planning" Questions

At the end of each session plan is a section entitled "Reflection and Planning." These questions are designed to guide your evaluation of that session. Take the time each week to consider these questions and discuss them with your co-leader. Your deliberate evaluation of your own leadership experience is the best way for you to recognize your strengths and weaknesses as a leader. Your co-leader can provide you with information about your behavior that you do not perceive, and you can offer similar information to your co-leader. Five or 10 minutes of reflection and discussion after each session can make a significant contribution to your growth as a leader. We urge you to make a commitment to this activity.

Several "Reflection and Planning" sections ask you to consider placing information about your group's activities in your congregation's newsletter. Discuss with your participants whether they wish to inform the congregation of some of their more noteworthy events in this way.

Leading Guided Imagery

Several sessions include guided imagery. This activity is particularly helpful in bringing intuitive knowledge to the conscious level. Intuition, by definition, is knowledge that resides in the unconscious and that comes to consciousness directly, without the mediation of reason. Guided imagery is a process that helps people gain access to their intuitive and imaginative potential and generate new and innovative patterns, hypotheses, and conceptions.

If you have not led this kind of activity before, practice a few times with your family or friends before leading your group.

In leading guided imagery, speak clearly yet soothingly, softly yet distinctly enough for everyone to hear you. Try to arrange your situation so your space will be quiet, darkened, and without interruptions as you lead these activities. If possible, have a room with a rug that people can lie on.

Be aware that while most high school-age people do see clear pictures in their imaginations, some do not. Those who do not see pictures, however, almost always experience other things; for example, feelings, sounds, body sensations, ideas, and awareness. Prior to the first guided imagery activity, ask participants not to have any specific expectations of this process, but simply to be open and pay attention to whatever comes into their awareness. Explain that in this context, imagery includes not only pictures but feelings, sounds, ideas, and so on, and that whatever comes into consciousness matters.

Projects

Note that Sessions 10 and 11 invite participants to plan and carry out significant projects. These projects may well be the most valuable and meaningful elements of this program.

Help the group plan and enact these projects in ways that are realistic and encourage success in both activities. There's no need to rush. Both projects can be done over a period of weeks or even months. Encourage the group to work on one project at a time, and see that participants assume an appropriate amount of leadership for these projects.

"Young Peacemakers" Video

An excellent new video to inspire young people to action is *Young Peacemakers* (EcuFilm, 1989, 20 minutes). This video helps young people see that peace is much more than the absence of war, and that they can have a positive effect on social change. The device of a video game introduces the stories of three teenagers who have become active peacemakers in their communities in a variety of ways.

Tonia Hutchinson, a 16-year-old black girl living in suburban St. Louis, is involved in many social activities through Students for Social Responsibility—including recycling and a hunger program. She has also initiated a black history class for children, held in her home.

Angel Perez is a 12-year-old Puerto-Rican boy who lives in one of the most violent and drug-infested areas of Brooklyn. At school he learned techniques of nonviolent conflict resolution and has become a mediator of conflicts whenever he encounters them. He demonstrates this skill of mediation to viewers, and he expresses his conviction that everyone can be a peacemaker regardless of circumstances.

Susan Goldberg is a Jewish girl of 14. She and others began the Los Angeles Students Coalition, which focuses on consciousness-raising and peaceful protests around such issues as homelessness, the grape boycott, and apartheid in South Africa. In the video, we see Susan and the students commemorating the birthday of Martin Luther King, Jr., by demonstrating against the abuse of children through apartheid.

Young Peacemakers can be purchased from EcuFilm, 810 Twelve Ave., South Nashville, Tennessee 37203, or rented from the UUA Audio-Visual Loan Library, 25 Beacon St., Boston, MA 02108-2800, (617) 742-2100.

Session 1 ♦ Exploring Peace and Justice–Part 1

Goals for Participants

- to explore the meanings and implications of the concepts of peace and justice
- to explore their awareness of themselves as peace-makers and justice-builders
- to gain an overview of this program.

Overview

This session engages participants in an initial exploration of the concepts of peace and justice. Participants are invited to (1) focus on these topics, (2) consider and articulate their existing knowledge and feelings about peace and justice, and (3) reflect on the knowledge and feelings expressed by their peers and by the leaders.

This session includes many different activities because one of its purposes is to involve participants in exploring peace and justice issues in a variety of ways. Keep the group moving along so that you have time to complete the session plan. If participants want to explore some issue in detail, you can restructure this plan, or you can explain that subsequent sessions provide for such detailed exploration.

Materials

- Newsprint, easel, markers, and tape
- 15' rope for the Tug of Peace
- Writing paper and pens or pencils
- Print materials such as books, magazines, flyers, newsletters, and reports for a Resource Table
- Chalice, candle, and matches

Preparation

- Set up a circle of chairs and/or cushions for the group.

- Have available an area where participants can lie comfortably on their backs for the guided imagery activity in the Integration. A clean, carpeted area removed from traffic is desirable.

- Set up the easel and newsprint.

- Set up the Resource Table with a collection of print materials related to the peace and justice issues the group will explore in this program.

- List each session number and title on a sheet of newsprint to be posted in the Closing.

Session Plan

Gathering   8-12 minutes

Greet participants individually as they arrive. Introduce yourself to anyone you do not know. Invite people to peruse the material on the Resource Table while the group gathers.

When the group has gathered, ask people to join you in a circle. Welcome the participants to this *In Our Hands: Senior High* peace and social justice program. Give participants a brief overview of the session.

Introduce the Rules for Sharing, as discussed in the Introduction to this program. Invite discussion about these rules. Then tell people that in a minute you are going to ask them to share the following with the group: their names, one thing that each of them is good at, and one special strength or skill that each has as a peace-maker. Give participants a little time to consider their responses, then offer your own responses, modeling the requested sharing. When you have finished, go around the circle having each participant share.

Interacting   10-15 minutes

Explain that you are going to engage the group in a "values line" as a way of beginning to explore the concepts of peace and justice. Draw an imaginary line across the room from one wall to another. Note that one end of the line represents complete agreement with a statement, while the other end represents complete disagreement. Explain that every other place on the line lies in relation to these two extremes. Be sure that participants understand how the line works and which end of the line holds which meaning.

Involve people in responding to the Values Line Statements — and to additional statements that you create — as follows:

- Read the statement aloud twice.

- Ask people to take a position on the line that reflects their degree of agreement with the statement.

- Once everyone is on the line, invite people to explain briefly why they chose to stand where they did.

- When all have shared who wish to do so, allow the sharing to evolve into a discussion, as time allows.

Values Line Statements

- Peace must begin with each person, with inner peace inside each person.

- If someone attacks me, then justice means that I have the right to strike back.

- Justice means that everyone is equal.

- You can't have peace without justice, or justice without peace.

- Peace is what you get when you don't have conflict or war.

Investigating   12-15 minutes

Gather the group in a circle. Then say something like: "One of the problems that people have had in working for peace over the years is that they haven't had a positive statement, a positive vision of what peace is. They've tended to define it as the absence of something — fighting, conflict, war, struggle — rather than the presence of something."

Invite reactions to this statement. Then have people organize into pairs. Ask each pair to discuss its ideas and feelings about what would be a positive vision of peace and to create a positive definition of peace. Hand out writing paper and pens or pencils. Say that you will ask them to share their definitions with the whole group.

Give the pairs about five minutes to talk. Then gather the group again, and have the pairs share their definitions. Invite reactions and discussion, as time allows.

Integrating   15-18 minutes

Tell participants that you are going to engage them in a guided imagery experience. Ask them to find a comfortable position, lying on their backs or sitting up with a straight back. Then ask people to close their eyes and take a couple of long, slow, deep breaths.

Lead this guided imagery by approximating the words below. Note that each ellipsis (three periods in a row) in these directions calls for a three- to five-second pause.

"I'd like you to breathe out now, and as you do, feel tension flowing out of your body...Now breathe in, and feel energy flowing in...Now breathe out...And now breathe in...Now I'd like you to tense your feet as much as you can...And let them go...And now tense the muscles in your legs...And let them go...Now feel the relaxation all the way from your feet to the top of your legs...Now tense your stomach...And let it go...And now tense your chest...And let it go...And now tense your back...And let it go...And now tense your hands, your arms, and your shoulders...And let them all go...And now feel the relaxation in your body all the way from your feet to your shoulders...And now feel that relaxation move up into your neck...Your jaw...Your face...And now all of your head.

"Now that you are calm and relaxed, you are going to go on a journey. Imagine now that you are walking along a stream in the woods. You're going upstream, making your way upwards, sometimes walking easily along the bank and other times scrambling on bare rock...The forest is all around you, tall green trees in every direction, yet you know where you are because you continue to walk up next to the stream...You're a little thirsty now after all this climbing, so you bend down to the water's edge and drink. The water is cold and delicious. There's no taste at all, just clear, cold water in your mouth. And you feel refreshed and ready to go on...Now you are walking upstream again. The stream is narrower here. The water is flowing faster, little rapids and waterfalls here and there...And you are still climbing, climbing up towards a very special place. You are almost there...Now you can hear it in the distance: the sound of gentle waterfalls, like a music of water and rock...Now you're very close. You can see this special place. It's a clearing in the woods, where three streams come together to make three waterfalls, surrounded by white birch trees. And now you know why you've come here. There is a teacher waiting here for you, your own teacher who will tell you something about your own potential to be a peace-maker or a justice-builder. Your teacher is waiting for you. You can see your teacher now, sitting on a rock next to the stream. Now I'd like you to go to your teacher and learn what this teacher has to tell you." (Pause for one minute.)

"Now it is time to go. You thank your teacher for the special message and say goodbye. And you start down the route you have come up, down along the stream...You're going downhill now, moving along effortlessly, almost like flying...Moving down and down and down, always along the stream...Now you are almost down again...Now you've made it. You're back where you started. And now I'd like you to come back to this room and whenever you are ready, to open your eyes. And when you have opened your eyes, I'd like you to consider what the teacher told you. And please remain silent while we are all doing this."

Give the participants a minute to reflect. Then ask them to divide into groups of three and share what they have experienced in their guided imageries.

After seven minutes, gather the whole group. Invite people to share any reflections or comments.

Closing   7-10 minutes

Post the newsprint poster of the list of sessions in this program. Explain that the first three sessions provide an introductory exploration of peace and justice issues and that then people will choose which of the other sessions they wish to experience. Be sure that everyone understands this structure. Then quickly go over the list of sessions.

Give the participants a brief preview of the next session. Invite people to bring in additional materials for the Resource Table.

Place the chalice in the center of the circle. Ask a participant to light it. As he or she does so, say something like the following:

"We light this light to signify the specialness of our circle of Unitarian Universalists — and to bring light to all that we have done and shared today."

Invite each person to share one insight or awareness that she or he has gained today. Remind people that they may pass if they wish. You may want to share first.

Ask people to stand. If they are comfortable with holding hands around the circle, have them do so. Engage the group in a moment of silence and/or singing an appropriate song. Then have a participant extinguish the candle. Close by playing the Tug of Peace as follows:

Move the group to an open space. Place the rope in a circle, with the ends overlapping. Have everyone — participants and leaders — seat themselves around the outside of the rope and grasp it. [Make sure the overlapping ends of the rope are held firmly.] Explain that the object of this game is for all of the members of the group to raise themselves to a standing position by pulling on the rope. If anyone falls, the group "loses." Ask for questions. Then count to three, and say, "Up!" Have the group try this several times.

Reflection and Planning

Consider these questions, and discuss them with your co-leader(s):

1. What parts of this session do I feel the best about? Why?

2. If I were to lead this session again, what would I do differently?

3. What preparation do I need to do for the next session?

Session 2 ♦ Exploring Peace and Justice–Part 2

Goals for Participants

- to further explore the meanings and implications of the concepts of peace and justice
- to explore their own attitudes and beliefs about a range of peace and justice issues
- to gain a greater awareness of the range of beliefs and attitudes that exist about peace and justice issues.

Overview

This session engages participants in further exploration of both the concepts of peace and justice and their own attitudes and beliefs about a variety of peace and justice issues.

Move your group through the activities in this session with the same tempo that you created in the first session.

Materials

- Newsprint, easel, markers, and tape
- Copies of Handout 1 ("Reaction Sheet"), Handout 2 ("Opinion Sheet"), and Handout 3 ("Incomplete Sentences")
- Three 3" x 5" notecards and a marker for each participant
- Pencils or pens
- Chalice, candle, and matches

Preparation

- Set up your usual circle and easel.

- Set up the Resource Table. If possible, add new materials. Invite members of your congregation who are active in the Unitarian Universalist Service Committee, the Unitarian Universalist United Nations Office, the Unitarian Universalist Peace Network, and your own social responsibility com-

mittee to bring in printed materials to share with the group through the Resource Table.

- Make copies of Handouts 1-3 for each participant.

- Read and reflect on the definitions of peace and justice listed below. Consider sharing these concepts with the group if they are not explored by the participants in discussion.

Peace is:

- the absence of war and violence
- the presence of justice and prosperity
- the creative management and resolution of conflict
- the condition of mutual respect
- the fruit of justice.

Justice is:

- the assurance of basic human rights
- the equitable distribution of resources
- the provision of deserved rewards and punishments
- the presence of cooperation and fair competition
- the requirement for peace.

Session Plan

Gathering   15 minutes

Greet participants as they arrive. Invite them to look at the materials on the Resource Table.

When the group has gathered, ask people to join you in a circle. Lead them in a brief checking-in. Then give participants a quick overview of this session.

Give everyone Handout 1 and a pencil or pen. Explain that you are going to read aloud 10 statements expressing opinions about peace and justice issues (see Handout 2). Ask participants to respond to each statement by making an X in one of the three boxes on the Reaction Sheet next to the number of that statement. Describe the three possible reactions as follows:

- The "thumbs up" means that you agree with the statement or approve of the value it conveys or implies.

- The "flat hand" means that you find roughly equal value on both sides of the issue, or that you don't fully understand the statement.

- The "thumbs down" means that you disagree with the statement, or disapprove of the value it conveys or implies.

Encourage people to record their first reaction upon hearing the statement. Explain that there is no necessarily "correct" response to any of these statements.

Read the first statement aloud twice, and then ask participants to mark their Reaction Sheets. Follow the same procedure with the other statements.

Interacting   15-20 minutes

Give each participant three 3" x 5" notecards and a marker. Show the group the three hands illustrated here, and ask them to draw a copy of each hand on a 3" x 5" card. Explain that they will use these cards to share with the group their reactions to certain statements.

Distribute copies of Handout 2 to everyone. Read the first statement aloud again, and ask people to hold up the card that represents their response. Ask a participant to tally the group's responses quickly, and announce the results; for example, "three agree, five neutral, six disagree."

Follow this procedure for all 10 statements, encouraging sharing and discussion in line with the following guidelines:

- For each statement on which there is disagreement, have one participant with a "majority view" and one with a "minority view" say a little more about his or her reaction.

- For at least a few of the statements, ask those who are sharing their reactions to do so without using any words. Ask them to pantomime or act out their reactions.

- For statements for which there is a wide range of response and much disagreement, have more than one person on each side of the issue share. Also seek divergent reasons for opinions by asking: "Does anyone agree or disagree for a different reason than someone has already shared?"

- Be sensitive to the possibility that some of the terms in these statements will not be familiar to all of your participants. Ask if people want terms defined, or ask for volunteers from the group to give definitions for terms that you think some participants do not understand. Be careful not to embarrass anyone as you do this.

Thumbs Up

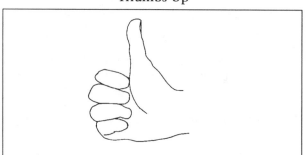

Thumbs Down

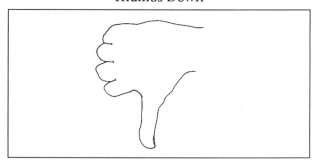

Flat Hand

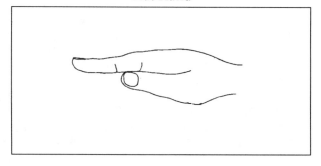

- Help to keep the interaction in the form of discussion, not debate or argument. If anyone becomes argumentative, ask them to share and discuss rather than debate or argue.

Be aware of the time as you lead the group through this activity. Encourage as much sharing as possible, but move the group through all 10 statements in the way described above.

Investigating   15-20 minutes

Hand out copies of Handout 3. Ask participants to read each of the incomplete sentences, consider how they would complete it, and jot down some key words about their completions in the spaces provided on the sheet.

Organize the group into four small groups. Assign one of the four incomplete sentences to each small group. Ask each group to discuss its sentence and generate and record a group completion to that sentence.

If there are fewer than eight participants, have two small groups, with one group addressing both peace statements and the other both justice statements.

Integrating   15 minutes

Gather the group in a circle, with participants sitting with members of their small group. Have participants who responded to the "ingredients of peace" statement share their completion. Invite responses as time allows.

Follow the same procedure with the other groups and other incomplete sentences.

Closing   5 minutes

Place the chalice in the center of the circle. Give participants a brief preview of the next session. Have a participant light the candle. Then say something like: "Let this light remind us of both the obstacles to peace and justice — and the ingredients of peace and justice."

Close with a standing circle, with participants joining hands, and a moment of silence and/or a song. Extinguish the candle. Hand out copies of Sessions 5 through 11 if you are planning to have individual participants describe these sessions to the group next time. Say goodbye to your participants.

Reflection and Planning

Consider these questions, and discuss them with your co-leader(s):

1. What was the best part of this session? Why?

2. What part of this session did I like the least? Why?

3. What preparation do I need to do for the next session?

Session 3 ◆ Making Choices

Goals for Participants

- to learn about the plans for Sessions 4 through 12
- to choose which sessions they wish to experience in this program.

Overview

The central activity is the participants' exploration of the plans for Sessions 4 through 11 and their selection of the sessions for the remainder of this program. To facilitate this process, be familiar with all the session plans so that you can describe them in a general way and respond to questions about them. While you probably don't need to read them word-for-word to attain this level of knowledge, you'll certainly need to look them over carefully prior to this session.

An alternative to your presenting the various sessions is to have each participant read over a session and describe it to the group. For this approach, you should have made a copy of Sessions 5 through 11, given out the session plans at the end of Session 2, and had people read them at home. (Plan to present Session 4 yourself, as it opens with a staged conflict that you do not want to reveal ahead of the session.) Or, have participants read over session plans at the beginning of this session.

Materials

- Newsprint, easel, markers, and tape
- Copy of the session posters, located at the back of this session
- Copies of Handout 4, "List of Sessions 4-12"
- Pens or pencils
- Eight small objects of the same kind for each participant, such as marbles, pennies, and pebbles
- Eight small paper bags
- Refreshments
- Chalice, candle, and matches

Preparation

- Set up your regular circle of chairs and/or cushions, and the newsprint and easel.

- Photocopy and post the session posters. Tape a paper bag below each poster.

- Photocopy Handout 4 for all participants.

- Skim the session plans for Sessions 4 through 12. Be prepared to describe each session in a general way. Remember to tell participants that Sessions 4 and 5 fit together to create a sequence about conflict. Be sure not to tell them about the staged conflict in Session 4.

- Bring simple refreshments for the Closing.

- Add to the Resource Table any new materials that you have gathered.

Session Plan

Gathering   12-18 minutes

Greet participants individually as they arrive. Invite them to examine the various session posters and allow them adequate time to do so.

When the group has gathered, begin with a brief checking-in. Then give people an overview of this session.

Engage participants in the cooperative game, Machine:

Ask one person to begin by standing alone in the center of the circle. Ask that person to make a repetitive action and a noise to go with it. Have the other group members join in one by one, each making a movement that relates in some way to another person's movement and each making a noise. When all have joined in, draw the group's attention to the "machine" they have created. Then call the "machine" to a halt.

Have the group discuss the following questions:

- What was the role of cooperation in creating the "machine"?

- What is the value of cooperation?

- What's hard about cooperating with other people?

If there is interest and time, have the group build a second "machine."

Interacting and Investigating   20-25 minutes

Gather participants in a circle, and say something like: "The purpose of the first two sessions was to get you thinking and feeling about peace and justice issues. Now it's your prerogative as a group to take the initiative and decide which of the other topics and areas in this program you want to explore."

Explain that you will present each of the session plans and respond to questions about them. Then the group will use a form of voting to decide what it wants to do.

Distribute copies of Handout 4, and the pens or pencils. Invite people to take any notes that will be helpful to them. Then refer to the poster for Session 4, and give a short description of that session. Invite questions about the session plan, and respond to them. Follow the same procedure for the remaining sessions.

When you have completed your discussion of Session 11, explain that Session 12 is a closing session that you will use to complete the *In Our Hands* program.

Give a brief introduction of the activities of this session.

Integrating   20-25 minutes

Explain that the voting will work as follows:

Each person will have eight votes. He or she can distribute these votes in any way that he or she chooses, from giving one to each session to giving all eight to a single session. When everyone has voted, the votes will be counted. Then the group will decide how many of the top vote-getting sessions they wish to do.

Be sure that everyone understands the voting process. Explain that there is time for a short "campaign" for the various sessions. Invite the participants to speak briefly to urge their peers to vote for a particular session. Encourage them to keep their speeches short and to the point.

When campaigning time is up, hand out eight small objects to each participant. Have people vote by placing objects in the paper bags under the session posters.

When all have voted, have participants count the votes. Then list on newsprint the sessions and the number of votes received in descending order. That is, list the highest vote-getter at the top of the sheet with the number of votes it received, the second highest below it, and so on.

When the list is complete, engage the group in examining the results and deciding how many of the "winning" sessions they wish to enact. Be sure that the group is guided in this decision by its voting. For example, if the top six sessions all receive more than 40 votes and the seventh one received only 14 votes, it would be logical to enact only the top six sessions.

When the group has reached agreement about which sessions to explore, ask the participants if they want to do these sessions in their current order or if they want to change the order. When you have come to an agreement, make a final list of the sessions in the order in which they will happen. Post the list. Then celebrate this achievement by bringing out the refreshments and inviting everyone to partake.

Closing   5 minutes

Gather the group in a circle. Give people a brief preview of the next session. Then place the chalice in the center of the circle, and have a participant light the candle.

Invite people to reflect on the candle's light for a minute. Then say something like: "Let the light of our chalice remind us of the brightness we create when we work together with others with cooperation and good feeling."

Close with a standing circle, hands joined, and/or with a song. Have a participant extinguish the candle. Say goodbye.

Note: If possible, leave the session posters on the wall throughout this program.

Reflection and Planning

Consider these questions, and discuss them with your co-leader (s)

1. How did things go in this session?

2. If I were going to lead this session again, what would I do differently? Why?

3. What preparation do I need for the next session?

Session 4:
What Is the Nature of Conflict?

- examine the nature of conflict

- identify the kinds of conflict we experience in our daily lives

- explore how people react to conflict situations

Session 5:

How Can We Manage Conflict and Resolve It Constructively?

- learn about handling conflict

- be exposed to various conflict management styles

- explore the win/win approach to conflict management

Session 6:
What Are Some Paths to Peace and Justice?

- identify four paths to peace and justice: strength, dialogue, law, and nonviolence

- examine our beliefs and values and these four paths

- be introduced to the beliefs of others and these four paths

Session 7:

How Do Unitarian Universalist Faith-Stances Relate to Peace and Justice Issues?

- define a faith-stance

- identify four common Unitarian Universalist faith-stances: humanism, theism, liberal Christianity, and mystical spirituality

- see how these faith-stances relate to peace and justice

Session 8:

Whom Do We Admire as Peace-Makers and Justice-Builders?

- meet historical figures who worked for peace and justice

- recognize the inspiration that these figures offer

Session 9:

What Peace and Justice Issues Face Our Generation?

- identify the important peace and justice issues facing our generation

- probe our understanding of and feelings about these issues

- explore one or more of these issues in greater depth

- refine our vision of a peaceful and just world

Session 10:
How Can We Act for Peace and Justice?

- identify four ways of acting for peace and justice: social education, social service, social witness, and social action

- take collective action for peace and justice

Session 11:

How Can We Promote Peace and Justice Through Worship?

- learn the structure and nature of worship

- choose to plan and lead a peace and justice worship

Session 4 ♦ What Is the Nature of Conflict?

Goals for Participants

- to explore the nature of conflict
- to identify and explore the kinds of conflict that they experience in their own lives
- to explore the role that they and others take in conflict situations.

Overview

Conflict is a normal and probably necessary element in human life. Conflict can motivate us to act, and to grow. Yet most of us perceive and experience conflict as negative and destructive.

This session and the following one offer the perspective that conflict in itself is neither positive nor negative; that it is the way we handle conflict that determines the quality of the conflictive experience. Often when we compete, avoid, or accommodate, conflicts become destructive. But when we can compromise and/or problem-solve, conflicts can become positive experiences that lead to satisfying outcomes.

Please note that you will need to recruit an adult accomplice, either another leader of this group or another adult who is known to this group, with whom you will stage a conflict. See the Preparation for details.

Materials

- Newsprint, easel, and markers
- Copies of Handout 5, "Conflict Behaviors"
- Pens or pencils
- Chalice, candle, and matches

Preparation

- Set up your regular circle of chairs and/or cushions and the newsprint and easel.

- Plan to stage a brief and realistic argument at the beginning of this session. Choose a conflict that is plausible, so that participants will be likely to perceive it as real. Discuss with your accomplice how the conflict will unfold. If you are working with a co-leader, stage the conflict with your co-leader. If you do not have a co-leader, recruit an adult from your congregation who is known by most of the group members to help you with the conflict. (For a discussion of enacting a "fake-fight," see page 57 in the LIFT Leaders' Guide.)

- Photocopy Handout 5 for all participants.

- Add to the Resource Table any new materials that you have gathered.

Session Plan

Gathering   5-8 minutes

Greet participants as they arrive. Invite them to peruse the Resource Table. When most or all of the participants have arrived, and just as you would usually gather the group in your circle, initiate the staged conflict with your accomplice.

Enact the conflict for several minutes. Then bring it to a halt, and let the people know — if they have not already guessed — that you were enacting a role play for the purpose of introducing this session's topic: conflict.

Interacting   10-15 minutes

Gather participants in a circle, and engage them in responding to these questions:

- What was going on in this conflict?

- What were the approaches or roles taken by the two people in the conflict?

- How did you feel while you were watching the conflict?

Move the discussion from this particular event to the larger issue of the nature of conflict by asking questions like:

- What is the nature of conflict?

- Is conflict necessarily destructive? Can it be constructive?

When appropriate, suggest to the group that conflict itself is inevitable, and intrinsically neither destructive nor constructive; that it is the way we deal with conflict that gives conflict its character. Invite responses to this perspective.

Investigating   20-25 minutes

If it feels appropriate, take a few minutes to have a brief checking-in. If not, omit this activity for this session. In either case, give participants an overview of the remainder of the session.

Organize your participants into small groups of three or four. Give each small group two sheets of newsprint and a marker. Print the following question on a sheet of newsprint: "What kind of conflict do you experience in your life?" Draw the participants' attention to this question. Ask people to discuss this question in their small groups and to write their responses on one sheet of newsprint. Have them print "Kinds of Conflict" at the top of that sheet.

After six to eight minutes, print the following question on your sheet of newsprint: "What are the causes of these conflicts?" Ask participants to discuss this second question, and to write their responses on their second sheet of newsprint. Have them print "Causes of Conflict" at the top of this sheet.

After another six to eight minutes, gather the whole group. Have each small group post its first sheet of newsprint and read its responses aloud. Encourage appropriate discussion.

Then follow the same procedure with the second sheet of newsprint. In both of these discussions, direct the conversation toward exploring the participants' understanding of the nature and causes of conflict in their lives. Also elicit their perceptions of the destructive and/or constructive qualities of the conflicts they experience and why they are destructive and/or constructive.

Integrating   12-20 minutes

Distribute copies of Handout 5 and the pens or pencils. Ask people to respond to the questions on this sheet. When they have done so, have them organize into groups of three and share their responses for two minutes.

Gather the whole group again. Invite people to share their overall reaction to the Conflict Behaviors form. As is helpful, ask questions like the following:

- What helps people to compromise when they are in conflict with each other?

- Is it realistic to expect people to problem-solve together if they are involved in a conflict?

- What happens when you'll do anything to avoid conflict?

- Can you share an example of a constructive conflict that you have experienced? What made it constructive? How could it have become destructive?

Closing   5 minutes

When time requires, end the discussion and give the group a preview of the next session. Then close in a way that is appropriate for your group, using the chalice and candle, words of reflection, joining hands in a circle, a song, and/or any other ritual elements that the group chooses. Say goodbye.

Reflection and Planning

Consider these questions, and discuss them with your co-leader(s):

1. What was good about this session? Why?

2. What was not so good about this session? Why?

3. How do I feel about the individuals in this group now? About this group as a whole?

4. What preparation do I need to do for the next session?

Session 5 ◆ How Can We Manage Conflict and Resolve It Constructively?

Goals for Participants

- to gain a greater awareness of their approaches to handling conflict in their own lives
- to learn about a variety of conflict management styles and the relationships among them
- to explore one method of creative conflict resolution: the win/win approach.

Overview

This session engages participants in exploring styles of conflict management and in learning about a creative method for conflict resolution, the win/win approach. Participants have an opportunity to enact some of these conflict management styles and the win/win approach through pantomime and role-plays.

The beliefs that underlie the activities of this session are the same ones articulated in the previous session: that conflict is a natural and inevitable element in human life; that conflict in itself is not necessarily destructive, but is directed in destructive or constructive ways by the styles that people use to manage and resolve conflict; and that the inevitability of conflict demands that we develop and learn constructive, nonviolent styles for managing and resolving conflicts.

Materials

- Newsprint, easel, markers, and tape
- Copies of Handout 6, "Conflict Management Styles," and Handout 7, "Guidelines for Win/Win Conflict Resolution"
- Pens or pencils
- Chalice, candle, and matches

Preparation

- Set up your usual circle and the easel and newsprint.

- Have an appropriate space for the guided imagery in the Initiation.

- Photocopy Handouts 6 and 7 for all participants.

- Make a newsprint poster of "Conflict Management Styles" (Handout 6).

- Set up the Resource Table.

Session Plan

Gathering   12-15 minutes

Greet participants individually as they arrive. Invite them to peruse the Resource Table.

When the group has gathered, ask people to join in a circle. Lead a brief checking-in. Then give participants a brief overview of this session.

Ask participants to take a comfortable position, lying on their backs or sitting up straight. Then say something like:

"Now I'd like you to relax. Take a couple of long, slow, deep breaths, and feel relaxation coming into your body each time you inhale...Breathe in slowly now...And now breathe out...And breathe in slowly...And breathe out...Once more, breathe in...And breathe out...And now I'd like you to tense the muscles in your feet, and hold them...And now let them relax...And now tense the muscles in your legs, and hold them...And now let them relax. Feel a wave of relaxation flowing from the soles of your feet up through your legs...And now tense your stomach muscles, and hold them...And let them relax...Now tense your chest muscles, and hold them...And let them relax...Now tense your back muscles, and hold them...And let them relax…Now feel that wave of relaxation moving up from your legs into your stomach and back, up your body…And now tense all of the muscles in your hands and arms, and hold them…And let them relax…Now tense your shoulder and neck muscles, and hold them…And let them relax…And now tense your jaw and face muscles, and hold them…And let them relax…Now feel that wave of relaxation moving up your arms and into your shoulders…And now feel it moving through your neck and your face and right up to the crown of your head…And now feel the relaxation all over your body." (Pause for 10 seconds.)

"Now I'd like you to recall a difficult or intense conflict that you have experienced recently and let yourself see what was going on in this conflict. What was this conflict about?" (Pause for 30 seconds.)

"And now I'd like you to let yourself see how you and the other person tried to resolve this conflict. What was your way or style of trying to resolve it? What was the other person's way or style? Let yourself see both of these." (Pause for 20 seconds.)

"And now I'd like you to imagine a way that you can bring this conflict to a resolution that is constructive and successful for both you and the other person. Let yourself imagine how this might happen." (Pause for 30 seconds.)

"Now I'd like you to bring yourself back to this room and, when you are ready, to open your eyes and carefully sit up. But please remain silent as you do this."

Interacting   8-10 minutes

Ask participants to organize into pairs and to share their guided imagery experiences with their partners for a few minutes. Tell people that you'd like each person to evaluate her or his partner's imagined constructive resolution to the conflict in terms of the following:

• Is it a constructive resolution to the conflict for both parties?

• Could it actually work?

When the partners have shared and responded, gather the whole group. Invite comments or questions about this experience.

Investigating   20-30 minutes

Note that the ways of resolving conflicts that people have discussed can be called "conflict management styles." Hand out copies of Handout 6, and post the newsprint-sized version in a central location.

Lead participants through an exploration of the Conflict Management Styles poster. First note the vertical axis and what it represents, then the horizontal one. Then engage people in considering each of the styles listed in the following order: avoid, accommodate, compete, persuade, encourage, compromise, and problem-solve. Have a participant discuss how each style relates to the two axes on the chart. Invite appropriate discussion to help participants understand the various styles and their relationship with each other.

When the group has considered the styles, organize your participants into seven pairs. (If you have fewer than 14 people in your group, organize as many pairs as you can. If you have more than 14 people, elicit volunteers.) Assign each pair a conflict management style without letting the other pairs know which style you have assigned. Ask the pairs to act out their style in pantomime for about 30 seconds. Give them one minute to prepare, and then have one pair begin. After the pair has completed its performance, ask the group to identify the pair's style. Then invite reactions and questions from the group. Follow this procedure with the other pairs and styles.

Then say something like: "In this model of conflict management styles, the style that is highest in both assertiveness — meeting your own needs — and in cooperativeness — meeting the other person's needs — is problem-solving. There are some guidelines for this kind of style that can help us to see how it might really work."

Distribute copies of Handout 7. Ask participants to read the guidelines, and then engage them in a discussion that clarifies their meaning and potential uses. If it seems useful, go over the steps in the Win/Win process one by one.

Integrating   15-20 minutes

Ask participants to offer examples of tough conflicts between people that they have personally experienced or observed. List their suggestions on a sheet of newsprint.

When there are several conflicts listed, ask for four volunteers to role-play the Win/Win approach to one of these conflicts. Have one participant or the group pick a conflict from the list. Tell the volunteers that there are four roles to be enacted: the two people as described in the conflict; and two advisers, one for each person in the conflict. Note that the rest of the group will serve as the audience. Explain the roles as follows:

- The two people in the conflict, called the role-players, are to role-play the conflict. They are to attempt to use the Win/Win approach to resolve the conflict.

- Each adviser is to pay close attention to her or his role-player. The adviser's goal is to help her or his role-player resolve the conflict successfully. Toward this goal, advisers can stop the role-play by saying "Freeze" whenever they want to give help or advice about the process to their role-players.

Ask each of the volunteers to choose a part for the role-play. Be sure they understand what they are to do. Then have the role-players begin.

At the conclusion of the role-play, thank the participants and have them rejoin the group. Then engage the group in reacting to the role-play. Focus the discussion on what they see as the strengths and limitations of the Win/Win approach. As part of the discussion, be sure to call on the role-players to share their experience.

As time allows, conduct a second and a third role-play, using the other conflict situations on your list.

Closing   5 minutes

When time requires, gather the group in a circle. Give participants a brief preview of the next session. Then close in a way that you and/or the group have chosen. You may want to include these words in your closing: "Let the light of our chalice remind us of our commitment as Unitarian Universalists to resolving conflict in a way that affirms the inherent worth and dignity of each person, and justice, equity, and compassion in human relations."

Reflection and Planning

Consider these questions, and discuss them with your co-leader(s):

1. What have I learned from the experience of leading this session?

2. If I were to lead this session again, what would I do differently?

3. What preparation do I need to do for the next session?

Session 6 ◆ What Are Some Paths to Peace and Justice?

Goals for Participants

- to explore four paths to peace and justice: strength, dialogue, law, and nonviolence
- to clarify their own beliefs and values in relation to these four paths
- to consider the beliefs and values of others.

Overview

This session engages participants in exploring four different paths to peace and justice that are commonly advocated and followed by governments, political and religious groups, and individuals throughout the world. The intent is not to present any one of these paths as necessarily better than the others, but to involve participants in considering and evaluating the arguments for and against the four paths.

Presumably, most people who are walking each of these paths genuinely believe they are seeking to promote peace and justice in the world. Yet those following one path often perceive those following another to be insincere or immoral. The approach of this session is to accept the premise of sincerity of those following each of the various paths, but to question the intrinsic value and effectiveness of each path. The activities of the session guide participants as they pursue these questions.

Please note that the exploration of the four paths does not focus on a particular level of human interaction (interpersonal, societal, and/or international), but leaves this decision to the participants and you. This breadth of scope encourages participants to pursue their own interests in relation to these four paths. However, this openness also creates the possibility of confusion, in that a discussion may move back and forth from one level of interaction to another without a clear understanding of what is being discussed. Be aware of this potential and help the group to stay focused on what it is exploring at any given moment.

Materials

- Newsprint, easel, tape, and markers
- Copies of Handout 8, "Four Paths to Peace and Justice," and Handout 9, "UU Principles and Purposes"
- Cardboard
- Writing paper and pens or pencils
- Chalice, candle, and matches

Preparation

- Set up your regular circle and easel.

- Have a table and five chairs available for the panel discussion in Integrating.

- Make four nameplates, by folding pieces of cardboard, that will sit up on a table. Print the name of each path on a nameplate.

- For the panel discussion, select a recent event or incident that involves a conflict related to peace and justice issues. For example, the US shooting down an Iranian airliner or youth gang violence in Los Angeles. Be able to describe this incident or event clearly.

- Bring in new materials for the Resource Table.

Session Plan

Gathering   12-18 minutes

Greet participants as they arrive. Invite them to peruse the Resource Table.

When the group has gathered, ask participants to join in a circle. Lead a brief checking-in. Give the group an overview of this session.

Print each of the four paths at the top of a sheet of newsprint, and post the four sheets. Say something like: "These are four different approaches or paths that people have used in their pursuit of peace and justice among individuals, groups, and nations."

Pick one path, and ask participants to try to define it. Record on newsprint the key words that they offer as definitions. Follow the same procedure with the three other paths.

Interacting   15-20 minutes

Hand out copies of Handout 8. Explain that these descriptions of the paths to peace and justice are not necessarily the "right answers" but, rather, offer additional explanatory material. Ask people to read them, then invite questions and comments.

When the group has discussed the Four Paths, ask participants to consider which path feels most valuable or worthwhile to them. Give them a minute to reflect, and then go around the circle, with each participant sharing her or his selection.

Please note that it is probably desirable for the leaders not to share their own opinions about the four paths at this time, so their values do not unduly influence the participants. The leaders can express their values later in the session.

When all have shared, have participants organize into small groups based on their selection of a most valuable path. If any group consists of a single person, have that person join another group.

Give each group writing paper, pens or pencils, a marker, and a sheet of newsprint. Distribute copies of Handout 9. Print the following questions on a sheet of newsprint, and ask each group to discuss the questions and write its responses on newsprint:

• What are the strengths of your path to peace and justice?

• What are the weaknesses of your path to peace and justice?

• What support can you find for your path in the UU Principles and Purposes?

Give the groups adequate time for discussion. Move from group to group, responding to any requests for clarification or assistance.

Investigating   15-20 minutes

Gather the small groups in a circle. Have one group post its sheet of responses and present them to the whole group. When the first small group has presented, invite other participants to raise questions and comments. Try to keep this inter-action a dis-

cussion rather than a debate. Follow the same procedure with the other small groups.

Integrating   15-20 minutes

Describe the structure of the following panel discussion, and have each small group pick one member to sit on the panel. When the panel members have been selected, have them sit in front of the group at the table, with the appropriate path nameplate before each one. Note that you will moderate the discussion.

Introduce the panel members and their paths, and describe the recent event that you have selected as an example of a real conflict. Then conduct a panel discussion in which each panel member is asked to respond to questions like:

• What insight does your path offer into this event?

• What solutions does your path offer in relation to this event?

When all of the panelists have shared their responses to these questions, give them an opportunity to respond to the comments of the other panelists. Afterward, thank your panelists for their participation.

Closing   5 minutes

Gather the group in a circle. Give participants a preview of the next session. Place the chalice in the center of the circle, and have a participant light it. Allow some moments of silence. Then say something like: "Let this light remind us that our understanding is always open to change and growth. Let me ask you to share with us, if you'd like to do so, some understanding that has changed or grown for you in our time together today."

Allow time for sharing. Then say goodbye.

Reflection and Planning

Consider these questions, and discuss them with your co-leader(s):

1. How did things go in this session?

2. What have I learned from the experience of leading this session?

3. What preparation do I need to do for the next session?

Session 7 ◆ How Do Unitarian Universalist Faith-Stances Relate to Peace and Justice Issues?

Goals for Participants

- to gain an introduction to the concept of faith-stances as an element in Unitarian Universalism
- to gain an introduction to four common Unitarian Universalist faith-stances — humanism, theism, liberal Christianity, and mystical spirituality
- to consider how these faith-stances relate to peace and justice issues.

Overview

This session requires the participation of four members of your congregation, each of whom (1) embodies a different one of the four Unitarian Universalist faith-stances presented in this session; (2) relates her or his faith-stance to peace and justice issues, concerns, and activities in her or his life; (3) is able and willing to discuss these matters with the group.

The success of this session is largely dependent on the quality of the guests whom you recruit. It is particularly important that your guests be able to converse with teens in an honest and open way. Ask your minister(s), religious education director, and/or social responsibility chair who might be appropriate to invite.

Materials

- Newsprint, easel, markers, and tape
- Copies of Handout 10, "Four Unitarian Universalist Faith-Stances"
- Nametags
- Chalice, candle, and matches

Preparation

- Set up the chairs or cushions in a semicircle facing four chairs or cushions for the guests.

- Set up the easel and newsprint.

- Have nametags or nametag materials for all participants, leaders, and guests.

- Photocopy Handout 10 for each participant, leader, and guest.

- When you have recruited four guests, meet with them prior to this session. Give each of them a copy of Handout 10, and ask them to be prepared to discuss the following questions: (1) How would you describe your faith-stance? (2) How does your faith-stance relate to your values about peace and justice? (3) In what ways has your faith-stance motivated you to action in peace and justice concerns?

- Let your guests know when and where your session will take place, and ask them to arrive ten minutes early.

- If you cannot find four appropriate people, you can go ahead with three faith-stance representatives, omitting the fourth or presenting it yourself.

- If necessary, it is possible to conduct this session effectively with volunteers role-playing one or two of the faith-stance positions.

Session Plan

Gathering   10 minutes

Greet guests and participants as they arrive. Ask everyone to make and wear nametags. Invite them to peruse the Resource Table.

When the group has gathered, ask people to sit in the chairs or cushions you have set up. Introduce the guests, and ask participants to introduce themselves to the guests. Give people a brief overview of this session.

Interacting and Investigating   35-45 minutes

Introduce the concept of a faith-stance within the context of Unitarian Universalism to your group. When you have done so, invite questions and respond.

Invite each guest to describe her or his faith-stance and to discuss how these religious beliefs and values motivate her or him toward beliefs and actions related to peace and justice issues. Give each guest five to seven minutes to talk.

You may want to have the group stretch between the second and third presentation.

When the guests have finished their presentations, invite participants to ask questions of the guests and the guests to reply. As much as possible, encourage that this interaction evolve into an informal group conversation. As part of this conversation, the guests may want to question each other. Encourage this unless it tends to place the participants into too passive a role.

Integrating   10-15 minutes

Distribute copies of Handout 10. Ask participants to read it, and invite comments and questions. Encourage discussion as time allows.

Closing   5 minutes

Move the chairs or cushions into a circle. Give participants a brief preview of the next session. Then place the chalice in the center of the circle, and have a participant light it. Allow a few moments of silence. Then invite participants and guests to share any observations or understandings that feel important to them now in light of the last hour's discussion. When all have shared who wish to do so, close with an appropriate ritual. Thank your guests for their participation, and say goodbye to the participants and guests.

Reflection and Planning

Consider these questions, and discuss them with your co-leader(s):

1. What was the best part of this session? Why?

2. What was the worst part of this session? Why?

3. What have I learned from the experience of leading this session?

4. What preparation do I need to do for the next session?

5. Does this group want to note any of this session's activities in our congregational newsletter?

Session 8 ♦ Whom Do We Admire As Peace-Makers and Justice-Builders?

Goals for Participants

- to gain a deeper understanding of several historical figures who worked for peace and justice in their lives
- to explore the inspiration that these figures offer them.

Overview

The format of this session is based on an old television program called "The Meeting of the Minds." Hosted by Steve Allen, it featured actors and actresses portraying well-known figures from various historical eras who engaged in fictional discussions of contemporary issues. For example, Aristotle, Machiavelli, and Emma Goldman might discuss the ethics of multinational corporations.

This session calls on you to organize a similar panel discussion about peace and justice issues. You play the moderator, and you enlist three to five volunteers from your group to enact the participants.

Please note that this session plan is structured differently from other sessions as follows:

- The panel discussion activity requires at least part of two meetings. Step One takes place in this session. Step Two will take place in the group's next meeting.

- Since the activities in Step One are not likely to require an hour, combine them with a social activity, new game, or another activity of the group's choosing. Note that for some of the time, the group will be engaged in this alternative activity while you meet with the panelists to prepare for Step Two.

Materials

For Step One

- Copies of "Panel Questions" (at the end of this session)
- Copies of "Profiles" (at the end of this session)

For Step Two

- Cardboard
- Pitcher of water and four glasses
- Costumes and props for the panelists

Preparation

For Step One

- Read and be familiar with the Profiles at the end of this session. Choose the ones you want to present to the group. If you wish, select other historical and contemporary figures, write profiles for them, and include them in this process.

- Photocopy each of the Profiles you will present to the group, and one copy of the Panel Questions for each panelist.

For Step Two

- For the panelists, set up a table and chairs facing the group.

- Make cardboard nameplates that will rest on the table, identifying the name of the character being portrayed, the dates of birth and death, and a descriptive phrase. Place the nameplates on the table in front of the chairs.

- Place the water glasses and pitcher on the table.

Session Plan

Step One

Plan to have a co-leader or guest engage the group in an interesting activity while you are meeting separately with the panelists.

If the group is very small, encourage every participant to be a panelist and consider making a presentation outside of this group, such as to parents, in church school, or in a worship service.

Consider arranging for someone to videotape or audiotape the panel discussion.

Gather participants in a circle, and begin with a checking-in and overview of this session. Then explain that you want to recruit three to five volunteers to take part in the panel discussion. Say something like: "I'm going to read short profiles of a number of well-known peace-makers and justice-builders, and I'd like you to think about which person interests you the most, which one you'd like to learn more about and portray in our panel discussion."

Explain that each volunteer will need to do a little research about her or his character before the panel discussion.

Then read aloud several excerpts from the Profiles you have selected.

Invite three to five volunteers to be panelists.

Engage the rest of the group in the alternate activity you have selected. Then gather the volunteers in a small group. Give each volunteer a copy of the Profile of her or his character and a copy of the Panel Questions. Explain that these questions are some of the ones that you will ask during the panel discussion and that you'd like the volunteers to do a little research about their characters in relation to these questions.

Discuss with the volunteers what costumes they will wear, and how they will create or obtain them.

Step Two (To take place at the group's next meeting)

1. Before this meeting, review the Profiles of the characters to be portrayed so that you can introduce them.
2. When the group meets for the panel discussion, gather all participants and begin with a checking-in and a brief overview.
3. Have the panelists take their positions, and begin the panel discussion by saying something like: "Welcome to this Meeting of the Minds. We're delighted that all of you can be with us today for this once-in-a-lifetime opportunity to hear from some of the great heroines and heroes for peace and justice in our history."

- Give a one-minute introduction of each character on the panel.

- Engage the panelists in discussion, using the Panel Questions as starting points. Encourage balanced time-sharing among the panelists.

- With about 20 minutes remaining in the session, ask for questions from the audience.

4. When time requires, thank your panelists for taking part and commend their efforts. Then invite the participants to reflect on and discuss in what ways these historical figures offer inspiration to them to care about peace and justice issues.

5. Close in a way that is appropriate for this group.

Reflection and Planning

Consider these questions, and discuss them with your co-leader(s):

1. How do I feel about this session?

2. What have I learned from the experience of this session?

3. What preparation do I need to do for the next session?

4. Does the group want to include information about the activities in this session in the congregation's newsletter?

Panel Questions

1. What are you most proud of as you look back over your life?

2. How did your religious beliefs and values affect the way you lived your life?

3. How can people create a more just and peaceful society?

4. What advice would you give to people today about working for peace and justice in their lives?

Jesus of Nazareth

(4 B.C.-A.D. 3 0)
"Lover of Enemies"

- Teacher, preacher, healer, religious revolutionary.

- Some of his teachings about peace and justice include:

    — The meek are blessed, because they will inherit the earth.
    — Those who suffer persecution for justice's sake are blessed, because theirs is the kingdom of heaven.
    — The peace-makers are blessed, because they will be called the children of God.
    — Everyone who is angry with his neighbor will be liable to judgment.
    — Judge not, that you be not judged.
    — Come to terms quickly with all your accusers.
    — Do not resist evildoers. If someone strikes you on the right cheek, turn to him the other cheek.
    — Love your enemies, do good to those who hate you, and pray for those who persecute you.
    — All that you wish others to do to you, do to them.
    — True prophets are known by their fruits.
    — Where your treasure is, there will your heart be also.
    — Sell what you have, and give to the poor.
    — Forgive those who have trespassed against you.
    — Love your neighbor as yourself.
    — The last will be first, and the first will be last.
    — To whom much is given, much will be asked.

Adin Ballou (Universalist)

(1803-1890)
"Pacifist Commune Founder"

- Minister, reformer, abolitionist, pacifist, founder of an experimental community called "Hopedale" in Massachusetts.

- Believed in putting ideals into practice — living, day by day, according to the principles of fairness, kindness, and peace.

- Initiated the Hopedale community as a practical expression of Christian faith — an attempt to live the "Law of Love" on a daily basis:

  — The simple religious life outlined by Jesus' teachings was their model: showing no hatred toward others, showing no loyalty to any power other than God, never lifting an angry hand against a neighbor, rejecting all forms of violence — especially war and its preparations — and sharing all property and profits equally.
  — The experiment was fairly successful during most of its 26-year duration, remaining pacifist throughout the American Civil War.
  — Hopedale was dissolved in 1868 after the two largest shareholders withdrew their funds, but Ballou considered this more a failure of morale.

- Ballou believed that the true liberation of the slaves would require a moral and spiritual conversion on the part of the people, rather than a military victory on behalf of the slaves.

- Ballou exchanged letters with the great Russian novelist and philosopher Leo Tolstoy, helping to shape Tolstoy's pacifist views.

Theodore Parker (Unitarian)

(1810-1860)
"Conscience of a Nation"

- Minister, scholar, reformer, abolitionist, shaper of the American democratic conscience and the modern Unitarian outlook.

- Suffered ostracism from his fellow Unitarian ministers because of his radical advocacy of religious freedom.

- Believed the liberal church — especially its young people — should take the lead in transforming society toward greater freedom and justice.

- Said we should follow the teachings of Jesus, not because of any special authority assigned to Jesus, but because his teachings are practical and uplifting in everyday life.

- Believed that war was inconsistent with the Christian message, and that most wars are morally abhorrent, but that in pursuit of justice, certain wars (such as the American Revolution) are justified.

- Denounced what he called the "social evils" of his time: slavery, restrictions on the freedom of women, low wages, bad housing, a press subservient to its advertisers, governmental decisions without the consent of the people, inadequate schools, inhumane prisons, and capital punishment.

- Parker saw religion as "natural" — not dependent for its truth or value on church, creed, or clergy.

- Advocated freedom for the human conscience and spirit beyond the shackles of external authorities and societal indignities.

- After he died, he was called "The Great American Preacher."

Henry David Thoreau (Unitarian)

(1817-1862)
"Civil Disobedience"

- Writer, teacher, naturalist, abolitionist, pacifist, and advocate of "civil disobedience"— disobeying the law according to the dictates of a higher inner law (conscience).

- His ideas about civil disobedience were a strong influence on Mohandas Gandhi, Rev. Martin Luther King Jr., Cesar Chavez, and many Vietnam War protestors and conscientious objectors.

- He spent one famous night in jail, following six years of refusal to pay taxes on the grounds that the government was engaged in two major injustices — slavery and the Mexican-American War.

- Some of his basic ideas include:

  — Each person should make known what kind of government would command her or his respect.
  — By respecting unjust laws, we become agents of injustice.
  — To serve a government with one's conscience is to resist it when it violates the higher moral law.
  — If we have unjustly taken a plank from a drowning man, we must give it back, even if it means drowning ourselves.
  — Many thousands are opposed to slavery and war in opinion, yet do nothing to put an end to them.
  — Since unjust laws exist, shall we obey them, amend them (and obey them until we have succeeded), or transgress them at once?
  — We meet government directly and face-to-face once each year in the person of its tax-collector, and paying taxes is supporting the governments policies, but are they just?
  — Under a government which imprisons any unjustly, the true place for a just person is also in prison.
  — A minority is powerless when it conforms to the majority, but it is irresistible when it uses its entire weight.
  — The best thing we can do when we are rich is carry out those schemes we had when we were poor.
  — A free and enlightened state recognizes the individual as the source of all its power and authority.

Julia Ward Howe (Unitarian)

(1819-1910)
"Mother's Peace Day"

- Feminist, patriot, abolitionist, civic leader, and peace-builder.

- Most remembered as the writer of the words to "The Battle Hymn of the Republic," but she preferred to be known as an advocate of women's cultural development, and as a prophet of world peace.

- Married Samuel Gridley Howe, a famous doctor and medical innovator who served the causes of education for the blind, improved conditions for the insane, and reform in public school.

- The Howes agreed on many social issues, but were at complete odds on the proper place of women in society. Julia was unwilling to live under any restrictions based on her sex.

- Saw civil war as a necessary crusade to save her country from the sin of slavery.

- Saw the elevation of the female half of the human race as the key to the progress of all.

- After the outbreak of the Franco-Prussian War in 1870, she became devoted to the cause of world peace.

- Believed that women, and especially mothers, were in an excellent position to avoid all the standard excuses for war, and thereby promote peace throughout society and among nations.

- As president of the Women's International Peace Association, she attempted to create a new holiday, "Mother's Peace Day," celebrating the natural leadership of women in giving birth to a world free of war.

Mary Livermore (Universalist)

(1820-1905)
"Untiring Reformer"

- Lecturer, writer, suffragist, abolitionist, and civic leader.

- Believed that the emancipation of women would do a great deal to cure the ills of society.

- With her husband, Daniel, she owned and edited a Universalist newspaper in Chicago, which championed reforms in the areas of abolition, temperance, and women's suffrage.

- During the Civil War, she worked for the Sanitary Commission, insisting that medical aid and other necessary supplies be sent to both sides in the struggle.

- After the war, she convened the first Women's Suffrage Convention in the state of Illinois, and then established a suffrage magazine, *The Agitator*.

- Beginning in 1870, she spent a quarter-century on the public lecture circuit, averaging 150 lectures per year, speaking primarily for the causes of women's rights, political education, and temperance.

- Her long and fulfilling partnership with her husband served as a constructive model for couples who aspire to work together for peace and justice.

Clara Barton (Universalist)

(1821-1905)
"Angel of the Battlefield"

- Teacher, feminist, nurse, administrator, founder of the American Red Cross.

- She taught for 17 years, founded a school in a poverty area, and resolved that if she were paid at all for her work, she would never do a man's work for less than a man's pay.

- She was opposed to slavery, but was not an abolitionist, believing that if the slaves were suddenly freed, more confusion would result, and so a more gradual solution was needed.

- During the Civil War, she was determined to go to the front lines to help alleviate the suffering of wounded soldiers on both sides of the battle lines, despite the fact that the front lines were not considered a fit place for women.

- The care system she developed was very efficient, following her own advice: "Think straight, plan carefully, and act boldly."

- By writing, lobbying, administrating, and providing direct service, she made sure that the clothing, blankets, medical supplies, and food arrived where it was needed — and become known as "The Angel of the Battlefield."

- After the war, and only a few days before President Lincoln's assassination, her project to search for missing soldiers was authorized.

- She described her experiences and discoveries on an exhausting speaking tour.

- On a rest trip in Europe, she learned about the International Red Cross, and determined that her country should participate. Upon returning, she began a 13-year campaign to persuade Congress.

- In 1881, her efforts gave birth to the American Red Cross, which she led for more than 20 years, responding to disasters in the US, Russia, Turkey, and Cuba.

William Howard Taft (Unitarian)

(1857-1930)
"Peace Through Law"

- International statesman, twenty-seventh President of the United States, tenth Chief Justice of the United States Supreme Court, and a Unitarian denominational leader.

- Believed that peace should be the goal of every nation, though war may be necessary as a step to achieve justice; and justice, in turn, enables us to build the foundation of lasting peace.

- After the Spanish-American War in 1898, he organized a colonial government for the Philippine Islands.

- Served as Secretary of War (now "Defense") under President Theodore Roosevelt.

- As President, Taft was a strong believer in national security, strict honesty in government, and conservation of natural resources.

- After his presidency, he promoted the "League to Enforce Peace," and later the "League of Nations" — believing that our best chance of achieving enduring peace is through an effective system of international law.

- Served as a Unitarian denominational leader for 16 years, during which time he convinced most Unitarians that Germany had become an evil force among nations, and that defeating her was essential to our hopes for a lasting and just world peace.

- He believed that high-sounding ideals are only useful when they lead directly to the kind of peace that can be enforced justly.

Mohandas Gandhi

(1869-1948)
"Nonviolent Liberator of India"

- Lawyer, protest organizer, civil disobedient, writer, commune founder, spiritual teacher, and peace-and-justice negotiator.

- Was very impressed with Jesus' teachings on nonviolence and Thoreau's teachings on civil disobedience.

- Aspired to become a "Karma Yogi" — a master of the path of action: firm in resolution, yet without egotism; respectful of others, but not afraid of them; very active, but not attached to the products or fruits of action; ever merciful and forgiving; neither puffed up by praise nor intimidated by criticism.

- Gandhi spent 22 years in South Africa, organizing the Indian congress, protesting discriminatory laws, establishing socialist communes, and writing articles on nonviolent protest while serving prison sentences.

- He spent his last 33 years in India, organizing for Indian home-rule and economic self-sufficiency, leading nonviolent protest campaigns, writing in prison, fasting against poor treatment of outcastes and against Hindu-Muslim violence, and negotiating with the British for Indian independence.

- Some of his basic principles of belief include:

  — We should refuse to cooperate with unjust laws.
  — All social evils, such as racial and ethnic discrimination, should be protested nonviolently.
  — People should live simply, and share their wealth equally.
  — To the greatest extent possible, we should refrain from harming all forms of life.
  — The rich should abstain from luxuries until the poor have enough.
  — The poorest of the poor ("outcastes" or "untouchables") are deserving of equal social standing, and should be called "Children of God."
  — "Peace Brigades" — trained groups of nonviolent volunteers — should anticipate and intervene in communal tensions, substituting for the police.
  — The truth (or essence) of human nature is revealed through loving actions.
  — "Truth-Force" is the practice of confronting and disobeying the upholders of unjust systems.
  — All principal religions contain truth and value, and their adherents should be respected.

Albert Schweitzer (Unitarian)

(1875-1965)
"Reverence for Life"

- Radical theologian, preacher, musician, philosopher, mission doctor, writer, advocate of nuclear disarmament, honorary member of the Church of the Larger Fellowship (Unitarian Universalist).

- Decided at the age of 21 to study religion, music, and philosophy, and to teach and preach, until the age of 30; and then to devote the rest of his life to the service of humanity.

- At the age of 30, he entered medical school, studied for eight years, continued writing books on religion and music, and then sailed for French Equatorial Africa with his wife, who had been trained as a nurse.

- Most of the next 30 years were given to his medical work with African families, although he still made time to write books on religion and philosophy.

- Some of his basic teachings include:

  — "Reverence for life" is the basis for the highest ethical system, as well as the basis for affirming life as it is; it is both an "ought" and an "is."
  — "Reverence for life" has a biological meaning — the instinct for survival; "I will to live."
  — It has a psychological meaning — the need to affirm and develop the creative potentialities of the self; "I will to live well, or more expansively."
  — It has a social meaning — the need to relate to and show concern for other's lives; "I will to live in the midst of others who will to live."
  — It also has a spiritual meaning — the concern for, and the need to connect with all life; "My will to live ultimately merges with the all will to live (the cosmos)."
  — We live ethically when we show reverence for life at various levels.
  — We cannot live without destroying life; therefore we must make careful judgments about what behaviors are most life-affirming, and least life-denying.
  — Those with "good fortune" (health, wealth, natural talents, a safe and nurturing environment) are obligated to help alleviate the suffering of those who are less fortunate.
  — God is the mysterious life-force, the forward-urging will in which all being is grounded.

John Haynes Holmes (Unitarian)

(1879-1964)
"Pacifism and Civil Rights"

- Preacher, pacifist, reformer, writer, organizer for civil rights, and Gandhi's chief American disciple.

- Served as minister of the Community Church of New York City for 42 years, during which time it became interracial and interfaith.

- Opposed all forms of violence, on moral and spiritual grounds.

- Was a staunch pacifist during both world wars, maintaining that our movement should help lead a "ministry of reconciliation" in the face of all international tensions, rising above the "taking of sides" and adding our knowledge and compassion to the cause of making a new world without war.

- Developed a new conception of the function of the church: it was to be a "revolutionary" force in the modern world, rectifying social ills and inspiring a devotion to world peace and justice.

- Held a vision of "nonsectarian religion" — a call to serve humanity that transcends cultural, racial, and creedal barriers.

- Made pioneering efforts in the areas of race relations, civil rights, social welfare, mental health, and birth control.

- Helped to found the National Association for the Advancement of Colored People (NAACP), the American Civil Liberties Union (ACLU), and the Unitarian Fellowship of Social Justice.

- In 1954, he was presented the Award for Distinguished Service to the Cause of Liberal Religions.

Albert Einstein

(1879-1955)
"Peace Through World Government"

- Scientist, writer, public speaker, pacifist, philosopher.

- Won the Nobel Prize in Physics in 1921, was appointed to the Intellectual Co-operation Organization of the League of Nations in 1922, and in succeeding years spoke in public many times (in Europe, Asia, and the United States) on social problems.

- Emigrated from Germany to the United States in 1933, and during World War II, co-operated with charitable organizations helping refugees to the U.S. from Nazi Germany.

- Pressured by the news that Nazi Germany was developing an atom bomb, he signed the famous letter to President Roosevelt encouraging the "Manhattan Project," which led to the development of the atom bomb.

- Some of Einstein's basic beliefs about peace and justice include:

  — There is only one path to peace and security — the path of supranational (world) government.
  — To abolish war, nations should hand over their sovereignty to a world government with a strong peacekeeping force.
  — "Patriotism" and "nationalism" are like hereditary diseases passed from generation to generation, encouraged by an alliance of heavy industry and the military.
  — The state transgresses its rightful powers when it forces citizens to engage in military service.
  — Conscientious objectors should be supported in their illegal struggles by an international organization.
  — As long as armies exist, any serious conflict will lead to war.
  — To kill in a war is not any better than murder.
  — The armament industry is one of the greatest dangers facing humanity;.
  — Nations will not disarm step by step; they will disarm all at once or not at all.
  — Do I fear the tyranny of world government? Of course, but I fear still more the coming of another war.
  — World government is certain to come; the only question is whether it will come before or after a nuclear war.
  — "Peace based on law" must gather behind it the force and zeal of a religion to succeed.

Dag Hammarskjold

(1905-1961)
"Spiritual Discipline and Peace-making"

- Economist, statesman, second Secretary General of the United Nations, mystic, and peace-maker.

- As a child he admired Albert Schweitzer's teachings on "reverence for life" and his service to humanity.

- He grew up believing that no life is more satisfactory than one of selfless service to one's country or humanity.

- As Secretary General, he worked successfully at resolving tense conflicts in Korea, the Middle East, and Central Africa — earning the esteem of many world leaders.

- One of his patterns of negotiation was to "elbow the superpowers out of the way" and then resolve the situation with the help of small powers.

- Some principles of his belief and action include:

  — All persons are equals as children of God.
  — Moral integrity (respect for law and truth) is the most persuasive force among nations.
  — Learn to see your adversaries objectively, but experience their struggles subjectively.
  — Fear of unpopularity is a major obstacle to true dialogue and diplomacy.
  — However primitive a basic cultural pattern may be, it has the seeds of a higher and more just pattern.
  — In our era, the road to holiness necessarily passes through the world of action.
  — The great mystics of the past found a way of self-surrender and self-realization, enabling them to say yes to their neighbor's demands, and yes to every fate life had in store for them.
  — Our secret creative will divines its counterpart in others.
  — Only those who truly listen can truly speak.
  — Pray for clarity of mind, so as to mirror life; and pray for purity of heart, so as to mold life.

- One of Hammarskjold's prayers was
  Give us a pure heart — that we may see thee
  A humble heart — that we may hear thee
  A heart of love — that we may serve thee
  A heart of faith — that we may live thee

- He was awarded the 1961 Nobel Peace Prize soon after his death.

Dana McLean Greeley (Unitarian Universalist)

(1908-1986)
"A Vision of Peace"

- Minister, denominational leader, social activist, founder of the world conference on religion and peace.

- As a youth and young adult he was an admirer of Theodore Parker and John Haynes Holmes — two very socially active Unitarian ministers.

- Served as minister of the Arlington Street Church in Boston for 23 years, and during the last four of these years, he served as the president of the Unitarian Service Committee.

- Served for eight years as the last president of the American Unitarian Association, and did much to facilitate the merger of the Unitarians and the Universalists.

- Served for eight years as the first president of the Unitarian Universalist Association, then as president of the International Association for Religious Freedom for two years, and then as minister of the First Parish in Concord for 16 years.

- His vision: "One world — open, committed, tolerant, dynamic and pluralistic, where people are seeking truth and unity all the time."

- Some of his principles of belief and action include:

  — We should have faith in peace, that it is good and that it is possible and that nothing in its place will suffice.
  — War is morally wrong from start to finish, and it must go if the human species is to remain.
  — We need to outgrow the idea that nations are sovereign above humanity.
  — Disarmament is the road to peace—nuclear disarmament primarily, but general disarmament secondarily.
  — The church must be the conscience of the state. There is a separation of church and state, but there cannot be a separation of religion and politics.
  — Social action is the fruit of religion, and the vehicle for the realization of a new world.

Lotta Hitschmanova (Unitarian)

(1909-   )
"International Relief"

- Journalist, humanitarian, founding director of Unitarian Service Committee of Canada, and public speaker.

- Forced to flee Czechoslovakia during World War II because of her strong anti-Nazi stand, arriving in Canada in 1942.

- Active in the American Unitarian Service Committee (USC) before arriving in Canada, she continued with European war-relief work from Ottawa.

- The need for a Canadian USC arose, and through energetic organizing, publicity, and fundraising, she was able to fulfill this need admirably. Explosive growth in her operation followed, with food, medical programs, education and vocational training, community development, and family planning services going to very needy children and adults in Europe, India, China, and Vietnam. The USC is especially known for its excellent care for orphans. Consistent with Unitarian principles, this aid has always been provided without regard for the religion, nationality, or ethnic group of those served. These efforts have won the deep praise and gratitude of thousands of recipients and dozens of leaders in the participating countries. Some of the early USC promotional literature reads: "When we are asked what Unitarianism means, we tell about the USC — our faith in action."

- The USC of Canada now draws its support from a very wide range of Canadian society, with only a relatively small percentage of the funding coming from Unitarians. However, Lotta Hitschmanova has said, "We keep the name 'Unitarian' in our title for historic reasons, and because the word expresses the oneness of humanity in which our organization passionately believes."

Mother Theresa

(1910-)
"Compassion for the Poorest of the Poor"

- Nun; missionary; teacher; nurse; founder of the Missionaries of Charity, which opened more than 70 centers (primarily in India) serving orphans, the jobless, the blind, the crippled, the retarded, the insane, the aged, people with leprosy, and the dying.

- While teaching and serving as a principal in a high school in Calcutta, she received "a call within a call" to help the poor while living among them.

- After three months of accelerated medical training, she opened a school and clinic for the poorest of the poor in Calcutta.

- Many donors, volunteers, and facilities came forth in response to her efforts, and the Missionaries of Charity became an official religious community in 1950.

- She organized followers in more than three dozen countries, and was awarded the 1979 Nobel Peace Prize.

- She says that her work is not "social work" so much as an effort to live out that life of love God has for his people.

- She says that welfare is for a purpose, whereas Christian love is for a person.

- In her centers, the dying receive the rituals they prefer — Ganges water on the lips for the Hindu, readings from the Koran for the Muslim, Last Rights for the Catholic.

- Her manner is humble and down-to-earth, yet self-assured and utterly practical. As one of her biographers described her, "She moves like a still point in a whirlpool of poverty and misery."

Martin Luther King

(1929-1968)
"A Dream of Justice"

- Preacher, scholar, writer, teacher of the philosophy of nonviolence, leader of the civil rights movement.

- Winner of the 1964 Nobel Peace Prize.

- As a young adult he studied the philosophy of nonviolence as presented in the writings of Gandhi and Thoreau, as well as the social ethics of several Protestant theologians.

- In 1955, Mrs. Rosa Parks refused to surrender her seat to a white passenger, and King became the leader of the Montgomery Improvement Association, which led the boycott of the public transit system.

- At that time he said, "We come here tonight to be saved from that patience that makes us patient with anything less than freedom and justice."

- Recognizing the need for a mass movement, he helped organize the Southern Christian Leadership Conference, giving him a base of operation and a national speaking platform.

- Guided by the philosophy of nonviolence, he helped organize many sit-in demonstrations and marches, protesting the economic, social, and political exploitation of black people.

- He said, "We know through painful experience that freedom is never voluntarily given by the oppressor; it must be demanded by the oppressed."

- He was sent to prison many times for his unwillingness to observe laws prejudicial to his people.

- In 1963, he helped organize the historic March on Washington, which included his famous "I Have a Dream" speech: "I have a dream that my four little children will one day live in a nation where they will not be judged by the color of their skin, but by the content of their character . . . ."

- These and other efforts had a strong influence on national opinion, gaining the support of Presidents Kennedy and Johnson, and resulting in the passage of the Civil Rights Act of 1964.

- The Poor People's March on Washington of 1968 was interrupted by his assassination. Only a week earlier he had said, "If a man has not found something he will die for, he is not fit to live."

- He regarded himself as "a drum major for justice, peace, and righteousness."

Session 9 ◆ What Peace and Justice Issues Face Our Generation?

Goals for Participants

- to identify what they perceive to be the most important peace and justice issues facing their generation
- to share their understanding of and feelings about these issues
- to choose to explore one or more of these issues in greater depth
- to reflect on a vision of a peaceful and just world.

Overview

This session helps participants identify what they think are the most important peace and justice issues their generation will face. The activities involve them in sharing their beliefs and feelings about the meanings and implications of these issues.

This session offers the group a springboard from which to create additional sessions. If participants wish to explore one or more issue(s) in greater depth, work with them to plan and enact additional sessions.

This topic may provoke powerful emotional responses from participants. Reflect on this possibility prior to the session and be prepared to be helpful and supportive in whatever ways are appropriate.

Materials

- Newsprint, easel, markers, and tape
- Copies of the poems by Josephides Panayiota (Handout 11) and Judy Chicago (Handout 12)
- Chalice, candle, and matches

Preparation

- Set up your regular circle and easel.
- Make copies of the two poems for each participant.

Session Plan

Gathering   12-15 minutes

Greet participants individually as they arrive. Invite them to peruse the Resource Table.

When the group has gathered, engage the participants in a brief checking-in. Give people a short overview of this session, and distribute Handout 11.

Note that the Panayiota poem was written by a 17-year-old from Cyprus. Have a volunteer read the poem aloud. Invite people to respond to the poem by asking questions like the following:

- Do you agree with the sentiment expressed in this poem? If so, why? If not, why not?

- What feelings do you have in reaction to this poem?

Keep this discussion brief, unless people express a strong desire to discuss the poem at length.

Interacting   15-20 minutes

Organize the group into sub-groups of three. Give each sub-group a marker and sheet of newsprint. Then say something like: "Many people see the times in which we live as a time of world crisis. We hear about different parts of the crisis almost every day in the news. There are so many issues and problems that sometimes it all feels overwhelming. But on the most basic level, it seems that all of these issues and problems can be seen as issues of peace and justice."

Invite reactions. Then say: "What I'd like you to do in your groups is discuss what you see as the most important, most critical issues of peace and justice that face the world today. Talk about this question for awhile — what the issues are, what the problems are — and then list the three or four most critical ones on your sheet of newsprint."

Be sure that participants understand the task. Then ask them to begin. Give them time to create their lists. When they have done so, have the groups post their lists on the wall.

Invite participants to examine all of the groups' lists. Then ask the group to create a new list that ranks the various issues according to how many times each one appears on the small group lists; for example, if "avoiding nuclear war" is on four lists and "preserving the Earth" is on three lists and no other issues are on more than two lists, the former is #1 and the latter is #2, and so on.

Investigating   20-25 minutes

Note the issue that is ranked first by the group. Tell participants that you are going to ask them to take part in a values line. Lay out the imaginary line as you did in Session 1. Then put the #1 issue as listed by the participants into the form of a question, as in this example: "What do you see as the likelihood of avoiding a nuclear war during your lifetime?"

Identify one end of the values line as "total confidence that nuclear war will be avoided" and the other end as "certainty that there will be a nuclear war." Be sure that participants understand what each point represents. Then repeat the question, asking people to take a place on the line that represents what they believe.

When participants have taken a position on the line, invite them to look at the distribution of the group. Encourage comments and reactions to this distribution, and encourage this interaction to become a discussion of the issue itself, as time allows. As part of this discussion, raise the following questions:

• What can people do about this issue or problem?

• What can we do about this issue or problem?

Follow this procedure with at least two more issues, as listed by the group. If time allows, explore others as well.

Engage the group in discussing the following question: "Are there ways in which these issues or problems are connected with each other?" If they

cannot do so themselves, help participants gain a sense of the relationships among various peace and justice issues.

Integrating   10 minutes

Engage participants in considering whether they would like to explore any of these issues in greater depth. If they would, begin to plan how the group will proceed.

You may need to complete this planning at the next session. With any additional sessions, involve participants in the planning and leadership as much as possible for your group.

Closing   5 minutes

End the discussion and give people a preview of the next session. Place the chalice in the center of the circle, and have a participant light it. Ask people to look at the flame for awhile and then close their eyes and allow themselves to become receptive. When all have had their eyes closed for awhile, tell them you are going to share a poem with them that you'd like them to reflect upon. Then read the Judy Chicago poem aloud.

Allow some moments of silence. Ask people to open their eyes. Close with a ritual that is appropriate for your group.

Pass out copies of the Judy Chicago poem as you say goodbye to the participants.

Reflection and Planning

Consider these questions, and discuss them with your co-leader(s):

1. How do I feel about the events of this session now?

2. Did any of the participants have experiences today that I want to follow up on in any way?

3. How do I feel about this group of people?

4. What preparation do I need to do for the next session?

Session 10 ◆ How Can We Act for Peace and Justice?

Goals for Participants

- to learn about four ways of acting for peace and justice: social education, social service, social witness, and social action
- to have an opportunity to plan and carry out a collective action for peace and justice.

If participants choose to engage in a project, they will:

- gain experience and skill in carrying out a project
- experience the commitment to other people and/ or to a cause that comes from planning and carrying out a project
- gain a sense of satisfaction and accomplishment from successfully enacting a project
- gain greater visibility and respect within their congregation.

Overview

This session introduces participants to four kinds of peace and justice activities: social education, social service, social witness, and social action. Participants explore these concepts and share their own experiences as examples of these activities.

The Integrating section invites the group to choose to enact a project that embodies one of these four kinds of peace and justice activities. The group will plan and carry out a social project only if they decide they wish to do so. Read the Preparation for guidelines for facilitating your group in such a project, and for an alternative if they choose not to undertake a project.

Materials

- Newsprint, easel, markers, and tape
- Copies of Handout 13, "Four Stories,"and Handout 14, "Four Ways of Acting for Peace and Justice"
- Pens or pencils
- Chalice, candle, and matches

Preparation

- Talk with appropriate members of your congregation prior to this session to see if there are existing projects within the congregation that your group might take on or join with as their peace and justice project. Be prepared to share this information with your group. An example is the "Walk for a Child's Future," coordinated by regional committees of the Unitarian Universalist Service Committee (UUSC) and carried out by members of local congregations. This activity includes both a witness component in its effort to raise public awareness about the anti-poverty efforts of the UUSC, and an indirect service component in its raising of funds to support these programs.

- Set up your usual circle and easel.

- Set up the Resource Table.

- Be prepared for the group's decision in the Integrating section

  — If participants decide to do a project, they spend the remainder of the session and, of course, considerable other time, planning and carrying it out.
  — If the group chooses not to do a project, Integrating includes another activity for the remainder of this session.
  — In either case, be prepared to answer the questions listed in Integrating.

- Please note that this session may motivate participants to want to carry out ambitious or multiple projects. Help participants keep their commitments at a realistic level. It is better to carry out a smaller project successfully than to start a more ambitious project that they cannot complete. Encourage them to work on one project at a time. However, if they wish to go on to a second project after completing the first one successfully, support this effort.

- For any project undertaken by the group, follow the guidelines below:

  — Provide leadership to the group as the participants select a project and begin to plan it.
  — As a part of the planning process, have the group identify a project chairperson, or cochairs, who will then take on the leadership role for this particular activity.
  — Provide support for the chair(s) and the group as needed throughout the project.
  — Enlist the support of interested and involved members of the congregation as appropriate and helpful.

Session Plan

Gathering   10-12 minutes

Greet participants individually as they arrive. Invite them to peruse the Resource Table.

When the group has gathered, ask people to join you in a circle. Engage them in a brief checking-in. Then give them a preview of this session.

Explain that the group will take part in a values line. "Draw" an imaginary line across the room, and designate one end as total agreement and the other end as total disagreement. Be sure everyone is clear about the meanings of the locations on the line. Then say something like: "I'd like you to respond to the following statement by taking a place on the line that expresses the extent of your agreement or disagreement with a statement. Here's the statement: 'There really is not much that I can do to make things more peaceful and just in the world.'"

When the participants have taken their places on the line, ask them to examine the distribution. Then invite people to explain briefly why they took the place they did.

Interacting   20-30 minutes

Explain that the group is going to hear four stories. Note that these stories are all true, although the names of the people and the settings have been fictionalized. Ask for a volunteer to read the first story. Give the volunteer a copy of Story A, and ask her or him to read it aloud. When the volunteer has finished reading, invite responses to the story.

Follow the same procedure with the other stories.

When the group has heard and discussed all of the stories, hand out copies of "Four Stories" (Handout 13) to all participants.

Investigating   15-20 minutes

Distribute copies of Handout 14. Ask people to read the entire sheet. Draw their attention to Social Education. Invite questions and comments, and respond as appropriate. When you feel that everyone understands the concept, ask participants to give examples from their own experiences that can be characterized as Social Education. Share from your experience as well.

Follow this procedure with the other three kinds of peace and justice activities, encouraging people to share their own experiences.

When the group has discussed all four kinds of activities, ask people to characterize the action that Sonia took in Story A in terms of these categories. Encourage discussion as appropriate.

Follow this procedure with the other three stories.

Integrating   10-20 minutes

Suggest the possibility that this group might plan and carry out a peace and justice project that represents one of the four categories: social education, social service, social action, or social witness. Note that a project could involve considerable time and effort, but could be both personally rewarding and meaningful to others. Engage the group in discussing this possibility. Help participants come to a consensus decision.

If the group wants to undertake a project, begin the process of selection as time allows. Three ways to proceed with this decision-making process follow:

- Involve the whole group in brainstorming a list of possible projects.

- Divide the group into small groups of three. Have each small group brainstorm a list of possible projects. Then gather the whole group, and have the small groups share their lists.

- Defer the selection process to another time, when you can involve a number of appropriate people from your congregation to talk with the group about possible projects—for example, someone active with the Unitarian Universalist Service Committee and with your congregation's social responsibility committee or members of your congregation who work in local or regional social education, social service, social witness, or social action agencies.

Whatever method you use to generate ideas, add any projects that you learned about from members of your congregation to the list.

Take this process of selection as far as you can in the time available. Then determine when the group will complete its decision-making and when it will act on its plan.

If the group does not want to undertake a project, acknowledge this decision. Devote any time remaining before the closing to a discussion of one or several of the following questions:

- What does our congregation's social responsibility committee do?

- What does the Unitarian Universalist Service Committee do?

- What does the Unitarian Universalist Peace Network do?

Closing   5 minutes

When time requires, gather your group in a circle. Give people a brief preview of the next session. Then close in an appropriate way. Say goodbye to the participants.

Reflection and Planning

Consider these questions, and discuss them with your co-leader(s):

1. What was good about this session? Not so good? Why?

2. If I were to lead this session again, what would I do differently?

3. What preparation do I need to do for the next session?

Session 11 ♦ How Can We Promote Peace and Justice Through Worship?

Goals for Participants

- to learn about the structure and nature of worship
- to have an opportunity to choose to plan and lead a worship service focused on a peace and justice theme.

If participants choose to lead a worship service, they will:

- gain experience and skill in planning and leading worship
- give creative expression to their concerns for peace and justice
- gain a greater understanding of and appreciation for worship as a way to engage and inspire people
- gain greater visibility and respect for their group within the congregation.

Overview

This session presents the group with an opportunity for public expression of their peace and justice concerns through the planning and leading of a worship service for youth and adults in your congregation.

If participants choose to experience this session but not to lead the worship service, they will learn more about how worship is organized and structured to engage and inspire people. This understanding can enrich their own retreats and conferences.

It is likely that some of the participants have already had experience in leading worship. One goal of this session is to help your participants gain the understanding that Unitarian Universalist worship can embody prophetic and/or advocacy dimensions, particularly in relation to peace and justice issues.

Materials

- Newsprint, easel, markers, and tape
- Copies of "Worship Meanings" (Handout 15), "Worship Components" (Handout 16), "Worship Resources" (Handout 17), and "Checklist for Service Leaders" (Handout 18)
- A calendar
- Chalice, candle, and matches

Preparation

- Set up the usual circle and easel.

- Set up the Resource Table.

- Make a newsprint-sized poster of the Sequence of Worship Planning, which appears at the end of this session.

- Make photocopies of Handouts 15, 16, 17, and 18 for each participant.

This session plan engages participants in a group planning process for much of the worship service that they will lead. This consensus process may be difficult if the group is too large. Do as much planning as possible with the whole group, and monitor the effectiveness of the process. If the group shows signs of getting stuck, suggest that it delegate some tasks to small groups or individuals.

Planning and preparing for a worship service cannot be completed in one session. Indeed, you may not even complete all of the other activities of this session plan in a single meeting. Be prepared to engage the group in scheduling the necessary preparation time for leading the worship service. You can remind them that if the task is worth doing, it's worth doing well!

Ideally, the group will lead its congregation's worship on Sunday morning. Prior to this session, discuss with the parish minister and worship committee (1) if this is possible and (2) if so, which date or dates are available. Mention that you will not know until after this session whether or not the youth will decide to lead a worship service, and that you will get back to them.

If possible, find a date three to six weeks after the group's commitment to this service. Fewer than three weeks will force you to rush, while more than six weeks will seem like a long time. If this time frame is not possible, consider having the group make its decision now, but delay the rest of this session until about a month before their service.

If no Sunday morning service is available, consider other options for a service, such as a special evening service, a congregational event, or a congregational retreat.

Session Plan

Gathering   18-25 minutes

Greet participants individually as they arrive. Invite them to peruse the Resource Table.

When the group has gathered, ask people to join you in a circle. Engage participants in a brief checking-in. Then give them an overview of this session.

Tell the group that you'd like to do a short guided imagery. Ask them to take comfortable positions, sitting up or lying on their backs. Ask them to close their eyes, relax, and take a couple of long, slow, deep breaths. Say something like:

"Now become aware of your feet, and feel the tension flowing out of your feet. Feel relaxation moving in...And now feel that relaxation moving up your legs...Now feel your stomach becoming loose and relaxed...And your chest...And your back...Now become aware of your fingers and your hands, and feel them relaxing...And feel that relaxation sweeping up into your arms...Up into your shoulders...And now into your neck...Now feel relaxation in your jaw...And your cheeks...And your eyes...And all of your face and head..."

"Now you are calm and relaxed all over...I'd like you to recall an experience that you've had of participating in a worship service, a service that really involved you, that really helped you to feel or understand something. Let the image of that service come into your mind's eye now." (Pause for 15 seconds.)

"Now I'd like you to look carefully at that service. Where was it?" (Pause for five seconds after each of the following questions.) "What was the mood of the service? What was the message? What

did you find inspiring or moving? What feeling did that service leave you with?" (Pause for 15 seconds.)

"Now I'd like you to return to this room and, when you are ready, to open your eyes and take your seat in the circle."

When participants are seated in the circle, invite people to share about the worship services that they recalled. As they talk about their experiences, ask people to notice if there are any common elements in the experiences shared. If so, list these elements on a sheet of newsprint.

When all have shared who wish to, distribute copies of Handout 15, "Worship Meanings." Ask participants to examine this material. Then invite them to make connections between the experiences they have shared and the information on this sheet. Encourage discussion.

After some discussion, say something like: "One traditional purpose of Unitarian Universalist worship is to educate people about issues of peace and justice: that is, to enlarge their awarenesses and arouse their consciences about such issues, and perhaps even call them to action. A project that we could take on as a group would be to plan a peace and justice worship service that we would lead for the adults and youth in our congregation. Would you like to do this?"

Note that planning and leading a service requires some time beyond today's session.

Invite questions and discussion. If appropriate, express your confidence that the group would enjoy planning and leading a service and would value the effort.

If there is a clear decision, help the group to state it and then move on in the session. If there is no clear decision, help the group move towards a consensus decision as quickly as it can.

If the group chooses to take on this project, praise them for their willingness to do so. If the group chooses not to take on this project, express your respect for this decision. Explain that you will lead them through as much of the planning of a peace and justice service as can be accomplished today as an exercise in learning about how to bring peace and justice issues into worship.

Interacting   15-20 minutes

Share with the group the result of your preliminary scheduling discussions with the parish minister and/or worship committee.

If possible, schedule the date (and time, if this is not self-evident) of the service now and confirm this date with the appropriate people after the session.

Display the newsprint-sized poster of the Sequence of Worship Planning. Briefly explain each item on the list to your group, and invite questions.

Post a sheet of newsprint labeled "Central Messages and Themes." Then say something like: "Let's brainstorm ideas for what the central message or theme of our worship service might be."

Review the rules for brainstorming. Then encourage suggestions. Write them on the newsprint yourself, or have a volunteer record them. The following questions may be used to prime the brainstorm:

- Do we want to raise a hope? a warning? a suggestion?

- What level of concern should we emphasize: personal? congregational? national? global?

- Do we want to address an immediate situation? a long-term issue? a broad theme?

- Do we want to raise questions? offer suggestions? both?

- What Unitarian Universalist principles and values do we want to address?

After five to eight minutes of brainstorming, or when participants have run out of suggestions, engage the group in reflecting on and discussing the suggestions. Help them sort through the suggestions and move toward a consensus choice.

Take as much time as needed to achieve a genuine consensus on the theme or message. At the same time, help the group move through this process within a reasonable amount of time.

When the group has articulated a consensus theme or message, write it on newsprint under "Central Messages and Themes." Congratulate the participants for achieving success in this process.

Investigating   10-20 minutes

Draw the group's attention back to the Sequence of Worship Planning. Note that the next step is components of the service. Hand out copies of Handout 16. Explain that this is a list of the elements or components found in a variety of Unitarian Universalist services. Note that no one service would include all of these components.

Quickly review the components. Ask participants to read the list of components individually and place a check next to the ones that they'd like to include in the service. Give them a minute or two to do this.

Involve the group in a discussion of which components they'd like to include in their service and in what order they would like to arrange them. It may be helpful to explain that for now they are just dealing with the kind of component — for example, a musical prelude, or a reading — and not the specific content of that component, such as the song "Give Peace a Chance," or several paragraphs from an essay by Lewis Thomas. Note that choosing the specific content of the worship components will come later in the process.

Use newsprint lists to help the group move toward agreement about which components to include and in what order. When agreement has been reached, list the components on newsprint as an order of service.

Integrating   15 minutes

Distribute copies of Handout 17, "Worship Resources," and Handout 18, "Checklist for Service Leaders." Ask participants to review them. If the group has chosen not to do the worship project, spend only a few minutes reviewing and discussing these two handouts before the Closing.

Involve the group in discussing the roles and tasks listed. Ask them what roles they will need for their service. Explain that this project will need someone to serve as chairperson. Briefly describe this role, then enlist a volunteer. The group also may choose to have co-chairpersons.

Closing   5 minutes

When time requires, gather the group in a circle. Schedule the next planning session for the service. If appropriate, give participants a brief preview of the next session.

Place the chalice in the center of the circle and have a participant light it. Say something like: "Let this chalice and its light remind us of the power of worship — to help us learn, to open us to caring and awareness and connection — and change."

Allow a moment of silence, then engage the group in an appropriate closing ritual.

Reflection and Planning

Consider these questions, and discuss them with your co-leader(s):

1. What was the most valuable part of this session? Why?

2. What was the least valuable part of this session? Why?

3. What did I learn from the experience of leading this session?

4. What preparation do I need to do for the next session?

5. Does the group want to note this session's activities in our congregational newsletter?

Additional Preparation for the Worship Service

At another time, the group will need to complete the following tasks:

- Choose the specific contents of the worship components, and fit the contents together into a coherent whole.

- Select a title.

- Write an Order of Service, and produce copies.

- Gather any desired materials and decorations.

- Complete any other planning and set-up.

- Have a full-scale rehearsal.

As much as possible, let the chairpersons lead the group through this process.

Sequence of Worship Planning

1. Message/theme

2. Components of service

3. Order of service

4. Roles

5. Title

Session 12 ♦ Celebrating What We've Done

Goals for Participants

- to explore the meaning of the terms "peace-maker" and "justice-builder" in light of their experience in this program
- to reflect on and make meaning of their experiences in this program
- to celebrate their experiences, understanding, and accomplishments in this program.

Overview

In this session participants reflect on, make meaning of, and celebrate their experiences and achievements in this program.

Hold this session at the very end of any peace and justice activities that your group has planned as direct outcomes of this program.

It would be a desirable addition to this session for the group to have lunch together after its conclusion, either at your congregation's building or in a restaurant.

Materials

- Newsprint, easel, markers, and tape
- Copies of Handout 19, "Questions for Reflection"
- Writing paper and pens or pencils
- Music
- A candle and holder for each participant and leader
- Lunch (optional)
- Chalice, candle, and matches

Preparation

- Set up your usual circle and easel.
- Photocopy Handout 19 for each participant.
- Prepare the candles and holders for use.
- Obtain a piece of joyous music to play at the beginning of the ceremony of celebration in the Integrating section.

Session Plan

Gathering   12-15 minutes

Greet participants individually as they arrive. When the group has gathered, ask people to join you in a circle. Have a brief checking-in, then give an overview of the session.

Tell the group that you are going to go around the circle, asking for one- or two-word reactions to a term. Ask people just to share their first response, without thinking about it. Print the term "Peace-Maker" on a sheet of newsprint, without allowing anyone to see the word. Then hold the newsprint up, and ask the person to your left to respond. Go around the circle two or three times, maintaining a quick pace.

Follow the same procedure for the term "Justice-Builder."

When you have completed the first reactions to the second term, raise the following questions and invite sharing:

- Do these two terms have any different meanings for you now than they did before this program? If so, how are they different?

- What feelings do you have about these terms now?

Interacting   18-20 minutes

Tell participants that you are going to involve them in a guided imagery. Be sure that everyone has a pen or pencil and a sheet of paper. Ask people to find a comfortable position, lying on their backs or sitting up, and close their eyes. Then lead the guided imagery by saying something like:

"Now take a couple of long, slow, deep breaths. In...And out...In...And out...In...And out...And now just let yourself breathe without directing it." (Pause for five seconds.)

"Now I'd like you to tense your feet as much as you can...And let them go...And now tense the muscles in your legs...And let them go...Now feel the relaxation all the way from your feet to the top of your legs...Now tense your stomach...And let it go...And now tense your chest...And let it go...And now tense your back...And let it go...And now tense your hands, your arms, and your shoulders...And let them all go. And now feel the relaxation in your body all the way from your feet to your shoulders...And now feel that relaxation move up into your neck...Your jaw...Your face...And now all of your head." (Pause for five seconds.)

"Now that you are calm and relaxed, I'd like you to see yourself in your mind's eye as you are today. See yourself as clearly as you can...And now let that image of yourself slowly, slowly begin to move forward in time...Now you are a year older than you are now... And now you have moved two years ahead...Now the pace is speeding up a little, and you are four years older...And now seven years older...And now you are ten years older than you are now, and you're still moving, though now you are slowing down...Slowing down...And now you have stopped. You are now 30 years old. Look at yourself in your mind's eye, and let yourself see what is there." (Pause for 10 seconds.)

"Now I want you to ask your 30-year-old self the following question and listen carefully for the reply: Who am I now as a peace-maker and justice-builder?" (Pause for one minute.)

"Now I'd like you to say goodbye to your 30-year-old self and begin to come back in time. Now you are moving. One year...Three years...You're picking up speed. Six years...Ten years now, and you are starting to slow down...You're still slowing down...And now you are back to the age you are today. And when you are ready, I'd like you to come back to this room and open your eyes. But please stay silent when you do this."

When all of the participants have opened their eyes, ask them to take a few minutes to reflect on their imagery experience. Invite them to write about their experience if they'd like to do so. Ask them to remain silent as they do this.

After four to five minutes, ask the participants to form pairs and to share with their partner whatever they would like about their imagery experience.

After six to eight minutes, gather the group in a circle. Invite people to share what they would like to about their imagery experience. If appropriate, raise a few questions to encourage discussion, but at the same time be sensitive to people's desires for privacy.

Investigating   18-25 minutes

Begin with the Human Chair, as follows: Have participants stand in a circle, side by side. Ask everyone to turn 90 degrees to the right, to bend their arms at a 90 degree angle, and to put their hands on each others' shoulders. Then say, "Sit down...gently!"

Point out that in this "human chair," we can all sit — and be sat on — and be perfectly comfortable. Relax and laugh in this position for awhile.

Have people stand, turn 180 degrees, and sit down again. Repeat the relaxing and laughing, and then stand up again.

Distribute copies of Handout 19. Tell people they will have about eight minutes to reflect on the questions and write some words in response to each.

Gather the group in a circle, and invite them to share their responses to the questions. Organize the sharing by addressing one question at a time.

Integrating and Closing   15-20 minutes

Tell the group that you want to close this session and this *In Our Hands* program by celebrating what everyone has learned and accomplished. Place the chalice in the center of the circle. Give each person a candle in a holder. Ask people to sit on the floor in a circle around the chalice. If possible, darken the room somewhat.

Tell people that you would like to engage them in a ceremony of celebration. Light the chalice, and play the joyous music. Say something like: "We have done much together in the last __ weeks; much that is worthy of celebrating."

Light your candle, and hold it before you. Go on to say: "I want to celebrate all of you in this group for (an accomplishment or discovery of the whole group, or whatever is appropriate in light of the group's experience). And I want to celebrate all of you for (another accomplishment or learning). And I also want to celebrate you for (another one)."

Continue in this manner as many times as is appropriate, given the group's experience. Place your candle a foot away from the chalice. Go on to say: "I want to ask each of you to celebrate something that you have accomplished or learned or done as a part of this group. To do this, I'd like you to take your candle, light it from the chalice, and say: 'I celebrate ___ ,' and name whatever it is that you want to celebrate today with us. If you want, feel free to name a couple of things. Then leave your candle a foot away from the chalice, so we make a circle of light around the chalice with our lights." Be sure everyone understands the procedure, then invite someone to begin.

When every participant who wants to speak has done so, read aloud this excerpt from a poem:

What will be the shape of our future?
The answer lies with us!
Let's join hands with peoples,
Peoples near and peoples far!

The shape of yesterday has been formed;
The shape of tomorrow is in our hands!

From R. Carroll Cannon, *Shaping Our Future Together* (San Diego: Torch Publications, 1984), 10-11.

Invite people to reflect on these words and on the circle of light. Allow a minute of silence.

Ask everyone in the group to stand and join hands. When all have done so, engage people in singing a song, if this is appropriate for your group.

Have everyone blow out the candles together. If appropriate for your group, close with a group hug.

Reflection and Evaluation

Consider these questions, and discuss them with your co-leader(s):

1. What are the most valuable gifts I have given during the course of this program?

2. What are the most valuable gifts I have received?

3. In what ways have I grown from the experience of leading this group?

Please photocopy the two-page evaluation form at the end of this book, fill it out, and send it to the UUA Curriculum Office.

Reaction Sheet

Thumbs Up	Flat Hand	Thumbs Down
1.		
2.		
3.		
4.		
5.		
6.		
7.		
8.		
9.		
10.		

Opinion Sheet

1. Given the way people really "tick," nuclear war seems inevitable.

2. Learning about the people of "enemy countries" makes war with those countries less likely.

3. High school students cannot significantly affect the state of peace and justice in the world.

4. We should support our nation's leaders, whether they are right or wrong.

5. The fact that nuclear weapons exist means that we must learn to settle conflicts among nations without war.

6. Peace and justice begin with each individual person.

7. It is possible for a country to win a nuclear war.

8. Humans need to learn how to interact with our natural environment in a peaceful and just way.

9. Without basic human rights, there can be no peace in a society.

10. The nuclear arms race is necessary as a deterrent to nuclear aggression.

Incomplete Sentences

I think the key ingredients of peace are...

I think the main obstacles to peace are...

I think the key ingredients of justice are...

I think the main obstacles to justice are...

List of Sessions 4-12

Session 4:   What Is the Nature of Conflict?

Session 5:   How Can We Manage Conflict and
Resolve It Constructively?

Session 6:   What Are Some Paths to Peace
and Justice?

Session 7:   How Do Unitarian Universalist
Faith-Stances Relate to Peace and Justice
Issues?

Session 8:   Whom Do We Admire As Peace-Makers
and Justice-Builders?

Session 9:   What Peace and Justice Issues Face
Our Generation?

Session 10: How Can We Act for Peace and Justice?

Session 11: How Can We Promote Peace and Justice
Through Worship?

Session 12: Celebrating What We've Done

Conflict Behaviors

Directions: In any conflict, most of us behave in a variety of ways. Each line below includes two opposite behaviors that people often use in a conflict. Read each line, and place a check in the box that best describes how you usually act in a conflict.

	MOSTLY	SOME OF EACH	MOSTLY	
Don't listen				Listen well
Present no new ideas about the issue				Offer ideas, alternatives
Are not interested in other person's view				Try to understand other person's view
Put down other person				Encourage other person
Don't want to hear about feelings				Ask others to express their feelings
Give in and let other person win				Keep working at a good solution
Fight it out verbally or physically				Stay calm
Try to change other one's mind				Pay attention to what other person is saying
Compete/want to win				Want to reach fair outcome
Avoid the issue				Work with the issue
Never give an inch				Are willing to compromise
Already know the answer				Want to problem-solve with other person

Conflict Management Styles

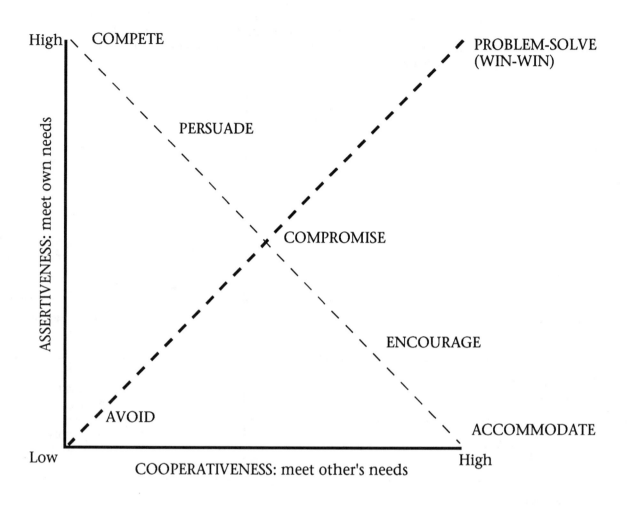

AVOID — Ignore the conflict, pretend it does not exist, run away from it.

ACCOMMODATE — Meet other's needs before your own; give in because you think the relationship is more important than your needs.

ENCOURAGE — Try to understand the other person's viewpoint and help or uphold him or her at the expense of your own needs.

COMPROMISE — Bargain, negotiate; both parties give up something of value.

PERSUADE — Try to talk the other person into changing her/his position or needs.

COMPETE — Try to win, to compel the other to accede to your will; meet your own needs, not the other person's.

PROBLEM-SOLVE (WIN-WIN) — Work together to find a solution that has the best results for both parties; requires genuine collaboration.

Guidelines for Win/Win Conflict Resolution

Win/Win conflict resolution means that the people in conflict work together to resolve the conflict. This approach is also called collaborative problem-solving.

The Win/Win aspect of this approach means that both parties in the conflict experience a significant element of success or winning in the outcome.

All parties to the conflict must take the following steps for this approach to work:

1. Let emotions cool down before you start to work on the conflict. All parties must be ready and willing to work on the problem in a reasonable way.

2. Define the problem together. State the conflict clearly and openly. Acknowledge the real differences that exist.

3. Share feelings and needs related to the conflict, and listen carefully to the feelings and needs shared by the other party. Before a conflict can be resolved to the satisfaction of both parties, each party must know fully the feelings and needs of the other and must believe that the other person knows about her or his feelings and needs.

4. Jointly gather information needed for resolution of the conflict. Doing this together gives validity to the information and gives both parties an opportunity to work together successfully.

5. Brainstorm and list as many options as possible that might resolve the conflict in a win/win manner. This is not always easy. The key is to state and record as many ideas or options as possible through brainstorming. Be as creative as you can. Include options that may seem unrealistic or even silly at first because they may lead somewhere.

6. Review all of the options raised, and select one by mutual consent. This assures shared commitment to the mutually developed and selected decision.

Two hints for using Win/Win approaches:

- Give the process enough time to work! Don't give up if it gets hard or takes considerable time. Remind yourself how valuable it will be to resolve the conflict successfully.

- Use humor whenever possible. Laughter frees people from fear, embarrassment, and anger, and creates a mood of hopefulness. It helps people to relax, let go of tension, and think more creatively and clearly.

Four Paths to Peace and Justice

The Path of Strength

Building up a strong force — military or personal — in hopes of discouraging attacks from others and thereby encouraging nonviolent solutions to conflict.

The Path of Dialogue Diplomacy

Advocating discussion and exchange of ideas and information before conflict begins; trying to negotiate agreements as a way of settling conflicts.

The Path of Law

Developing laws or treaties that set up procedures for settling conflicts among people or nations and then following these procedures when there is a conflict; in the case of nations, getting as many nations as possible to sign and obey treaties.

The Path of Nonviolence

Living a spiritually oriented lifestyle that affirms basic human worth and dignity and refuses to participate in personal violence or the support of violence by institutions or nations.

UU Principles and Purposes

We, the member congregations of the Unitarian Universalist Association, covenant to affirm and promote

- The inherent worth and dignity of every person;
- Justice, equity and compassion in human relations;
- Acceptance of one another and encouragement to spiritual growth in our congregations;
- A free and responsible search for truth and meaning;
- The right of conscience and the use of the democratic process within our congregations and in society at large;
- The goal of world community with peace, liberty and justice for all;
- Respect for the interdependent web of all existence of which we are a part.

The living tradition we share draws from many sources:

- Direct experience of that transcending mystery and wonder, affirmed in all cultures, which moves us to a renewal of the spirit and an openness to the forces which create and uphold life;
- Words and deeds of prophetic women and men which challenge us to confront powers and structures of evil with justice, compassion and the transforming power of love;
- Wisdom from the world's religions which inspires us in our ethical and spiritual life;
- Jewish and Christian teachings which call us to respond to God's love by loving our neighbors as ourselves;
- Humanist teachings which counsel us to heed the guidance of reason and the results of science, and warn us against idolatries of the mind and spirit.

Grateful for the religious pluralism which enriches and ennobles our faith, we are inspired to deepen our understanding and expand our vision. As free congregations we enter into this covenant, promising to one another our mutual trust and support.

Purposes

The Unitarian Universalist Association shall devote its resources to and exercise its corporate powers for religious, educational and humanitarian purposes. The primary purpose of the Association is to serve the needs of its member congregations, organize new congregations, extend and strengthen Unitarian Universalist institutions, and implement its principles.

(Adopted as a Bylaw by the 1984 and 1985 General Assemblies.)

Four Unitarian Universalist Faith-Stances

Humanism

Turning away from a focus on "God" and building a faith in human abilities and ideals to establish a better life in a more humane world.

UU Principle: "...teachings which counsel us to heed the guidance of reason and the results of science, and warn us against idolatries of the mind and spirit..."

Humanists may be devoted to peace and justice because they affirm that:

- as human beings, we are creatures of inherent worth and dignity

- human beings alone are responsible for making our world better

- democratic and scientific methods will ultimately work to improve living conditions for all.

Theism

Questing for the divine, as expressed in many different religious traditions, and developing a faith in God or the creative life-force, enabling us to open ourselves to spiritual transformation.

UU Principle: "Wisdom from the worlds' religions which inspires us in our ethical and spiritual life..."

Theists may be devoted to peace and justice because they affirm that:

- the divine spirit is in all people

- God is the common ground underlying all cultural and religious differences

- it is our highest calling to bless the creation.

Liberal Christianity

Finding unique spiritual power in the ministry of Jesus, and embracing a commitment to follow him, while reappraising the Gospel through the insights of modern culture.

UU Principle: "Jewish and Christian teachings which call us to respond to God's love by loving our neighbors as ourselves..."

Liberal Christians may be devoted to peace and justice because they affirm that:

- love is the best way to cooperate with God's hope for humanity

- Jesus was committed to helping the poor and the oppressed

- Jesus taught us to love our enemies.

Mystical Spirituality

Disciplined effort to awaken to the sacred oneness or reality, both within and beyond ourselves, thus bringing balance and wholeness to personal life and the social order.

UU Principles: "Respect for the interdependent web of all existence of which we are a part...Direct experience of that transcending mystery and wonder, affirmed in all cultures, which moves us to a renewal of the spirit and an openness to the forces which create and uphold life..."

Those with mystical-spiritual orientation may be devoted to peace and justice because they affirm that:

- inner peace is the beginning of world peace

- hurting others is really hurting ourselves, because we are all interconnected

- violence is forgetting our common origin and forsaking our common destiny.

Poem

The world is like a crystal ball ready
to smash into pieces at any moment.
We, the young generation,
hold the ball in our hands.
We mustn't let it crash.
We can bring love and peace.
We can fight for this. We can keep
the ball still. Well, let's fight.
We are holding the world in our hands.
We can stop war and hate and bring
back the missing love.
Yes, we can, because life and the
world belong to us.

By Josephides Panayiota, age 17

From *My World-Peace*, edited by Richard and Helen Exley.

Poem

And then all that has divided us will merge
And then compassion will be wedded to power
And then softness will come to a world that is harsh and kind
And then both men and women will be gentle
And then both men and women will be strong
And then no person will be subject to another's will
And then all will be rich and free and varied
And then the greed of some will give way to the need of many
And then all will share equally in the Earth's abundance
And then all will care for the weak and sick and old
And then all will nourish the young
And then all will cherish life's creatures
And then all will live in harmony with each other and the Earth
And then everywhere will be called Eden once again

By Judy Chicago

From *Peace: A Dream Unfolding*, edited by Patrick Crean and Penny Kome.

Four Stories

These stories are true. Only the names of the people and some details of the settings have been changed.

Story A

Sonia was almost 16 when her sister, Natalie, became pregnant. Natalie was two years older than Sonia. Sonia was shocked because she knew Natalie had planned to go to college when she graduated from high school in three months. But now Natalie was telling everyone that she was engaged to Dan, and they were going to be married before the baby was born.

Sonia tried to talk sense with her sister. She felt very deeply that it would be a mistake for Natalie to become a mother now, to give up her potential for a college education and a good career. But Natalie wouldn't listen to her or anyone else. At one point in one of her many talks with Natalie about this subject, Natalie had confessed to her that her pregnancy was really a mistake in the beginning, although she swore up and down that now she was happy about it. Natalie explained that she had become pregnant because she hadn't really understood how birth control worked.

Sonia was astounded all over again. Here was her older sister who was supposed to be smarter and know more — and yet Sonia had to explain to her about her fertility cycle and the different kinds of birth control, all after the fact, when it was too late.

Sonia couldn't convince Natalie to change her mind, but her frustration motivated her to start an educational program at the the Southside Community Center. She enlisted a youth counselor and a nurse, both women, and worked with them to set up a three-hour course called "Knowing My Body" that included education about fertility and birth control. Then she went out and recruited her friends and acquaintances to take the course. After a few meetings, word of the course spread not only through Sonia's high school but also through two other high schools in town. Because of Sonia's efforts, more than 200 young women gained more control over their own lives in a single year.

Story B

Nathan was a high school junior. Most of the time he was reasonably content, but sometimes he felt guilty because he was so comfortable and there were so many people in the world, even in his own country, for whom life was hard. He didn't have to worry about any of his basic needs or even about having ample spending money for late-night snacks with his friends, for CD's, and for software for his computer.

But Nathan read a lot, whatever he could get his hands on. And he knew a lot about the world, about the thousands of infants and children who died from dehydration or malnutrition every single week of the year, about the millions of people who went to bed hungry at night, if they had a bed, about the millions and millions of people who had no safe supply of water. It was an endless list of needs. And when he let himself think about this, it felt as if it might drive him crazy. "But there's nothing I can do about it," he'd say to himself. "I'm just one kid."

One day Nathan read in the newspaper about a group that was building homes in his town for people who had become homeless. They were looking for volunteers to help them. They could use anyone who wanted to work, whatever skills they had. At first Nathan passed quickly over the story once he knew what it was about. But then something in it caught him, and he read it again. Here was something real he could do, he thought. He was good at building things, at using tools skillfully. He could really help these people. All he had to do was want to do it.

It took him three days to decide to volunteer. Within two weeks he was working on the construction project two afternoons a week and much of Saturday. He could already do a lot of what was needed — carrying, carpentry, nailing — and he learned a lot more about putting up wall board and installing pipe for plumbing. The work went on for more than four months, and when it ended, and the families moved in, Nathan felt that he had really done something that mattered. It didn't change the whole world, but it certainly helped some real people in need.

Story C

Kate was depressed about all of the nuclear weapons in the world. "Why did I have to be born at this crazy time of the world?" she wondered. She thought it was all so stupid and insane: all of these old men who already lived most their lives wanted to blow up the Earth, and for what? There was nothing that was worth fighting about so much that it should end up in a nuclear war.

The previous week in her world history class, her teacher had explained why the United States had dropped the atomic bomb on Hiroshima and Nagasaki at the end of World War II. He had justified it by saying that it had ended the war with Japan. But that didn't really feel right to her. How could the United States, a nation that was supposed to care about the rights and the values of people, be the first — and only — country to use the bomb?

Kate felt frustrated by all of this. Most of her friends didn't even want to talk about it. They just said, "Well, there's nothing you can do anyway, so why worry about it? Better to ignore it all." But she couldn't ignore it for long.

One Sunday at her church she saw a poster announcing a vigil at the office of her local Member of Parliament (MP). He had supported the government policy that had allowed the US to test cruise missiles in the Canadian Arctic. The only purpose for cruise missiles was to deliver nuclear weapons. An interfaith group that disagreed with this policy was planning to protest by spending 24 hours in silent witness before his local office. It would be a legal protest, with all the necessary permits.

Kate had never done anything like this before, but she felt drawn to this action in a way that surprised her. She called up the number on the poster and learned all about the vigil. It would begin at noon and last for 24 hours.

Kate made an agreement with herself to participate, even though part of her was reluctant to take this kind of a public stand. On the day before the vigil she made her sign. It said: "Nuclear Weapons Can Kill Us All. Stop the Madness Before It's Too Late. Say No to Cruise Testing!" The next day she joined about 60 other people from all over the province who gathered for this vigil. For 24 hours she sang, talked, sat or stood in silence, and shared food with five dozen people she had never met before. They all helped each other stay awake and warm through the long, chilly night.

In the morning, a TV camera crew came to take some footage of the vigil and interview a few of the people for the evening news. A little later, one of the MP's aides came to talk with the group, and they had an emotional discussion. She had spoken twice, which amazed her since she was usually uncomfortable talking in large groups.

At noon, the vigil ended. She said goodbye to the people she had met and went home. When she talked about her experience with her parents later that day, she said, "Well, I guess I don't think that it's going to make nuclear bombs go away or anything. But I do feel a little more hopeful now, because I feel like maybe there is something that people can do that will make a difference sometime."

Story D

David was a senior in high school in 1969. He had been appointed editor of the school newspaper the previous spring. But now he was frustrated with the whole situation. He had written an editorial in which he called the war in Vietnam stupid and pointless, not to mention hypocritical. Yet when Miss Jacquin, the faculty advisor, had read the editorial, she had warned him that it might not be a good idea to publish it. He had insisted. She had explained that while she didn't disagree with what he had to say, the school paper might not be the right place to say it.

"Why don't you send this as a letter to the editor of the *Herald*?" she had asked.

"No," David had replied. "This is where I want to publish it."

Eventually, Miss Jacquin referred the editorial to the school principal, Mr. Campbell. And when he read the editorial, he hit the ceiling. "You'll print this editorial in this school when hell freezes over," Mr. Campbell told David.

But it all seemed wrong to David. Why couldn't he publish it? Why didn't the right of freedom of expression apply to him as well as anyone else? Or to people in school as well as adults?

David's response to the principal's ultimatum was to found an alternative school newspaper. With the help of some friends, he printed up a couple of hundred copies of a four-page paper, including his editorial. Yet as he was giving away copies of the paper in front of the cafeteria, Mr. Campbell accosted him, seized the copies, and suspended him from school for a week.

David was outraged. He told his story to a lawyer at the American Civil Liberties Union, who agreed to take his case to court. It took 18 months — and by that time David was a sophomore in college — but he won his case in federal district court. And more importantly, he won the right of freedom of the press for school newspapers in the United States. The precedent that his case set was the standard of law for almost 20 years, until the US Supreme Court, in 1988, limited the rights won in David's case.

Four Ways of Acting for Peace and Justice

Social Education: Acting in a way that causes others to become more aware and more knowledgeable about a problem, issue, or situation. Social education is based on the belief that when people are educated about a problem, issue, or situation, they will be more able and more likely to act in relation to it.

Social Service: Acting in a way that offers immediate aid or help to those who need such assistance; an immediate response to the needs of those who are suffering.

Social Witness: Acting in a way that makes a clear moral and/or political statement about an issue, problem, or situation. Social witness is based on the belief that both people like oneself and people who are in power may respond to clear, powerful expressions of feeling and belief.

Social Action: Acting in a way that directly changes a structure, law, or system that is violent and/or unjust so that it becomes more peaceful and/or just.

Worship Meanings

Some of the basic meanings of Unitarian Universalist worship:

"worth-ship" shaping things of worth

celebrating life showing reverence for life

seeking inspiration openness to wonder, awe, mystery

appeal to conscience devotion to improving quality of life

commitment to righting a wrong re-connecting to creative power, or God

Unitarian Universalist Association

Worship Components

Traditional Items

Opening Words
Hymns
Song of Aspiration
Chalice Lighting
Responsive Readings
Announcements
Offeratory
Closing Words

Speaking

Sermon
Sharing
Panel
Guests

Ritual

Candles
Flowers
Communion
Passages

Visuals

Centerpieces
Sculpture
Artwork
Natural Objects
Wall Hangings
Banners
Slide-shows

Singing

Congregational
Choral Anthems
Duets
Solos

Reading

Common
Antiphonal
Scripture
Affirmation
Poetry
Writings

Drama

Scene from Play
Theatrical Readings
Skit

Music

Prelude
Interlude
Postlude
Instrumentals
Recordings

Centering

Meditation
Prayer
Silence
Bells
Gongs

Dance/Movement

Individual
Group
Joining Hands
Hugging

Worship Resources

Songs

Hymns in New Form for Common Worship. Boston: UUA, 1982.
Hymns for the Celebration of Life. Boston: UUA, 1964.
Hymns for Living. London: Lindsey Press, 1985.
Songs for a Friendly Planet. Evelyn Weis, ed. New York: Riverside Church, 1986.

Readings

Readings for Common Worship. Boston: UUA, 1981.
My World-Peace. Lincolnwood, IL: Passport Books, 1985 (pp. 116-127).
Peace: A Dream Unfolding. Patrick Crean and Penny Kome, eds. San Francisco: Sierra Club Books, 1986.

Guides

Youth Sunday: Approaches That Work. Pat Schwing. Boston: UUA, 1982.
Leading Congregations in Worship: A Guide. Boston: UUA, 1983.

Checklist for Service Leaders

The service leader is not directly responsible for all of these tasks, but the leader should make sure that all tasks are carried out by someone.

Before Sunday

_____ Plan Order of Service.

_____ Call musician(s) and plan music, including hymns.

_____ Include names of ushers, greeters, musicians, flower arrangers, etc. in the Order of Service.

_____ Arrange for Order of Service to be reproduced.

_____ Decide which tasks to delegate and ask others to carry them out.

_____ Call Minister or President to see if there are special announcements.

_____ If children will be present, consult with religious education leader.

_____ Practice reading through the service so sequence and words are familiar. Check pronunciation of unfamiliar words.

_____ Be sure decorations have been planned (flowers, art objects, banners).

_____ Plan to arrive well before the service begins.

Before the Service

_____ Check heat and air conditioning.

_____ Check lighting and sound system.

_____ Check placement of chairs, lectern, hymnbooks, Orders of Service.

_____ Check placement of all decorations.

_____ Check placement of chalice or candle, matches.

_____ Be sure offering baskets/plates are at hand.

_____ Check to see if last-minute announcements need to be read.

_____ Check whether illness, death, or other important events need to be mentioned.

_____ Be sure ushers and/or greeters are present. If not, draft some.

_____ Sound bell, gong, or other signal a few minutes before service time.

_____ Signal prelude to begin.

_____ Take your seat, enjoy the music and setting, relax.

After the Service

_____ Be available to greet people and be responsive to their comments about the service.

_____ Thank those who helped with the service.

Questions for Reflection

The most important things I have learned/gained in this program are...

Our group has helped me by...

I wish this program...

Today I...

Unitarian Universalist Association

Evaluation of *In Our Hands: Senior High*

We Need You! Help us serve you by sending us your comments, suggestions, and critiques. Please photocopy this form, using additional sheets if needed, and send your evaluations to: Curriculum Development Office, Unitarian Universalist Association, 25 Beacon Street, Boston, MA 02108-2800.

General Information

1. With what age group did you use this curriculum?

2. Approximately how many participants?

3. How many leaders?

4. Anything else you would like to tell us about your religious education setting (very small or very large society, etc.)?

General Comments

It would be helpful if you include comments on what worked and what didn't and how you modified the program to fit your needs.

Comments on Sessions

Session 1: Exploring Peace and Justice—Part 1

Session 2: Exploring Peace and Justice—Part 2

Session 3: Making Choices

Session 4: What Is the Nature of Conflict?

Session 5: How Can We Manage Conflict and Resolve It Constructively?

Session 6: What Are Some Paths to Peace and Justice?

Session 7: How Do Unitarian Universalist Faith-Stances Relate to Peace and Justice Issues?

Session 8: Whom Do We Admire As Peace-Makers and Justice-Builders?

Session 9: What Peace and Justice Issues Face Our Generation?

Session 10: How Can We Act for Peace and Justice?

Session 11: How Can We Promote Peace and Justice Through Worship?

Session 12: Celebrating What We've Done

Unitarian Universalist Association